Mairi Morrison MacDonald MacIver
Stornoway   Isle of Lewis
Scotland.

Bonnie Prince Charlie

Herman Macleod Paulson
Stornoway   Isle of Lewis
Scotland

Bonnie Prince Charlie

BONNIE PRINCE CHARLIE

On the engraving, within the oval border:

CHARLES EDOUARD, FILS AINE DE JACQUES STUARD, NÉ A ROME, LE 31 Decembre 1720.

Gravé par J. Daullé graveur du Roy. 1744

PRINCE CHARLES AT TWENTY-FOUR
From an engraving by J. Daullé
British Museum

Fr.

BONNIE PRINCE CHARLIE

By

CLENNELL WILKINSON

Author of
" Nelson " " The English Adventurers "
" William Dampier " etc.

LONDON
GEORGE G. HARRAP & CO. LTD.
BOMBAY & SYDNEY

First published October 1932
by GEORGE G. HARRAP & CO. LTD.
39-41 *Parker Street, Kingsway, London, W.C.*2
Reprinted October 1932

Printed in Great Britain by Wyman & Sons, Ltd.,
London, Fakenham, and Reading

PREFACE

If it be alleged against this book that it is slight the answer is, perhaps, that the subject is slight. Prince Charles would have made a good king, because he had the simple, kingly virtues. It was permitted to him only to be a pretender. He is great, not for what he was, nor even for what he did, but for what he stands for. To have given the world a new romance is an achievement which we may all rank differently, according to our temperaments; but surely no ordinary man could have done it. That reflection seems to put in their place the Lord George Murrays, the Cumberlands and Elchos, and Charles's other enemies and critics, each of whom has a well-earned paragraph in the history books—and no more. The romantic tradition which Charles founded is a subject worthy of abler pens than mine. But it is not my subject—which is Bonnie Prince Charlie, the young adventurer, himself.

Prince Charles was pretender to a throne, but he never in his life pretended to anything else. All the rest of his stock-in-trade—his vivid personality, his sportsmanship, his admirable directness of thought and action—was entirely his own. So was the tradition he left behind him—for even Robert Burns could not make bricks without straw. He failed to save England: he was too late. He failed to save the clan system: he was just too late for that. But he saved the kilt and the tartan and the songs of Scotland and the very soul of the Highlands. And he died a disappointed man, believing himself a failure, never knowing how much treasure he had rescued from the wreck.

As far as possible I have avoided footnotes, and have given references only when it seemed unavoidable. In these circumstances it seems desirable to acknowledge my principal authorities here. I have, of course, drawn heavily upon the following: *The Lyon in Mourning*, by the Rev. Robert Forbes (edited by Henry Paton, Edinburgh, 1895–96); *Itinerary of Prince Charles Edward Stuart*, by Walter Biggar Blaikie (Edinburgh, 1897); *Origins of the Forty-five*, edited by Walter Biggar Blaikie (Edinburgh, 1916); *Jacobite Memoirs of the Rebellion of 1745*, by the Right Rev. Robert Forbes (edited by Robert Chambers, Edinburgh, 1834); *A Short Account of the Affairs of Scotland in the Years* 1744, 1745, 1746, by David Lord Elcho (edited by the Hon. Evan Charteris, Edinburgh, 1907); *Memoirs of the Rebellion in* 1745 *and* 1746, by the Chevalier de Johnstone (London, 1820); *Memorials of John Murray of Broughton*, edited by R. F. Bell (Edinburgh, 1898); *The History of the Rebellion*, by John Home (London, 1802); *Narrative of Charles Prince of Wales' Expedition to Scotland in the Year* 1745, by James Maxwell of Kirkconnell (Edinburgh, 1841); *The Lockhart Papers* (London, 1817); *Culloden Papers* (London, 1815).

Then there are the State Papers and the Stuart Papers at Windsor. Lord George Murray's own narrative is in the *Jacobite Memoirs* mentioned above, and Captain Daniel's in Blaikie's *Origins of the Forty-five*. Crichton, the Edinburgh Whig, tells his story in *The Woodhouselee MS.* (edited by A. F. Stewart, London, 1907). The *Cochrane Correspondence* (Glasgow, 1836) is useful for the Jacobite occupation of Glasgow, and Dr Carlyle's story of Prestonpans will be found in his *Autobiography* (edited by John Hill Burton, London, 1860). The best modern lives of the Prince are those of A. C. Ewald and Andrew Lang. I should also like to mention two quite new books, Sir Charles Petrie's *The Jacobite Movement* (Eyre and Spottiswoode, 1932), and Miss Audrey Cunningham's *The Loyal Clans* (Cambridge University Press, 1932), which have given me great pleasure and assistance.

These have been my principal authorities during two years of desultory and much interrupted reading. I have only to add my personal thanks to Sir Charles Petrie, Mr George Blake, and Mr G. M. Thomson for many friendly and helpful suggestions. And perhaps I should apologize for being an Englishman.

C.W.

CONTENTS

ILLUSTRATIONS

MAPS AND PLANS

Charles. R.

BONNIE PRINCE CHARLIE

CHAPTER I

THE RESCUE PARTY

It was a wild and dirty night in Innsbruck, on the 2nd of April, 1719. Snow had fallen earlier in the day, and now sleet and rain together descended upon the picturesque old town in a merciless downpour, so that the gutters which ran down the centre of each narrow cobbled street were turned into torrents of muddy water, mingled with all the refuse of the town, thrown casually from upper windows, as was the custom in those days. The foot passengers in sight hastened upon their business, keeping close to the walls for shelter, their cloaks muffled about their ears. At the Black Eagle Inn, which occupied an inconspicuous site somewhat removed from the centre of the town, the storm beat savagely upon the shuttered windows, and the few inhabitants who had sought temporary refuge there crouched together over the fire, cursing the unseasonable weather.

In one of the private rooms of the inn, dimly lit by a few flickering candles, a party of newly arrived travellers sat in silence—evidently listening and waiting for something. They whispered nervously among themselves. Where was their leader ? He was already half an hour overdue. What could have gone wrong ? This business of rescuing distressed princesses was not so easy as it had sounded at Strasbourg when they gathered together over a bottle of wine in the regimental mess, concocting their plans. So said one of the two men present to his male companion, dropping his voice still lower at the word "princesses," and glancing anxiously towards the women-folk in the background.

The speaker was a fine figure of a man, tall, square-shouldered, blue-eyed. His companion was older, aged about fifty, fat and short of breath, but carrying himself with a certain dignity and—what was more surprising—with an air of thoroughly enjoying the whole business. He has left us by far the liveliest account of this strange adventure [1]—for it is time to confess that this story I am telling is no romantic fiction, but an even more romantic fact. Both men were splashed with mud from head to foot, their wigs all awry, and water streaming from their boots—so that one of them said afterwards that they must have looked more like brigands than a princess's escort. They carried large muffs, as was the fashion of the time, hugging them to their breasts and warming their hands in them. Underneath the mud and the muffs could be seen the uniform of Dillon's Irish regiment, that famous fighting force of exiled Jacobites which had already distinguished itself by its deeds of valour in the French service, and was now doing garrison duty at Strasbourg just across the frontier. The short, stout officer was named Major Richard Gaydon, and the taller and younger, with the dare-devil blue eyes, was Ensign Lucius O'Toole.

It was now some weeks since they had first been brought into this adventure, almost before they realized what was happening to them. Upon the sleepy garrison town of Strasbourg there had suddenly descended that mad Irishman the Chevalier Charles Wogan, bubbling over with a new scheme. Wogan was Gaydon's nephew. Of

---

[1] Now in the British Museum. For English translation see Sir J. T. Gilbert's *Narratives of the Detention . . . of Clementina Stuart* (Dublin, 1894), and for Wogan's version *Female Fortitude*, by Charles Wogan (London, 1722).

all the Irish adventurers then roaming the Continent he was the most reckless, and his eloquence was the most irresistible. Wogan, as a boy of eighteen, had been out in the Fifteen, and had been taken prisoner at Preston and incarcerated in Newgate Gaol, with no apparent prospect before him but a messy death on the scaffold. He broke out somehow, for he had a natural genius for escapes, and hid in the house of a friend. London was being combed for escaped Jacobites, and on one occasion Wogan had to take refuge on a roof in broad daylight with an angry Whig mob in the street below—or that was his own story: he was a great boaster. Anyhow he got clean away to France, and entered the service of the Old Pretender, James III, at Rome.

He was now on a new and more romantic adventure— so he told his uncle Gaydon at Strasbourg—something that no Irish gentleman would care to miss. It was, indeed, so wildly romantic that if he had been talking to Englishmen they would probably have disbelieved him. After the failure of the Fifteen the Old Pretender, who was then a man of about thirty and unmarried, had realized that if he waited until he was seated on the throne of England before seeking a bride he might very well die a bachelor, thus allowing the direct line of the Stuarts to die out. Glancing round the Courts of Europe, his rather cold and calculating eye fell upon the charming Princess Clementina Sobieski, granddaughter of the Polish hero who had saved Europe from the Turkish menace at the siege of Vienna in 1683. James wrote to his friend Colonel Dillon, of the Irish Regiment, asking for advice, and it was Dillon who had recommended his relative Wogan as a suitable emissary.

So Wogan had been to Silesia. He had won over Prince and Princess Sobieski, father and mother, to his cause, and had found the little Princess quite delighted

13

at the prospect of becoming a queen. He had got her and her mother actually started on their journey to Italy, and had even brought James to Bologna to wait for them there. He had accomplished all this, and there seemed nothing more to do except to warn the bell-ringers, when the devastating news arrived that the Hanoverians had heard of the proposed marriage, the English Government had protested to the Emperor, and the two Princesses had been stopped at Innsbruck, in the Emperor's territory, and detained there, politely but strictly guarded. The problem now was to rescue Clementina from durance vile, and escort her across the Italian border, and so into the arms of her waiting lover. It is astonishing that so unromantic and businesslike a person as James should ever have listened to this madcap scheme. But he did. And Prince Sobieski, after protesting at first that "the time had gone by for such Don Quixote adventures," yielded in his turn to Wogan's impassioned eloquence and gave his consent.

And Wogan had been to Innsbruck; and had seen the palace where the Princesses were detained; and had got into touch with a certain M. Chateaudoux, gentleman-usher to the elder Princess Sobieski; and had discovered that this Chateaudoux was in the habit of introducing women into the palace any night that he liked, with the connivance of the porter; and had arranged with him to bring a rescue party to the town, consisting of not more than four cavaliers (lest their numbers should attract attention) and one servant-girl (who was to take the place of Chateaudoux's inamorata and change clothes with the Princess Clementina, so that the latter might slip out unchallenged); and had conveyed all this to the Princess, who had agreed to the plan on condition that another lady was added to the party to keep her company in the flight to Italy.

14

THE OLD PRETENDER
Scottish National Portrait Gallery
Photo Annan, Glasgow

14

That was the story which Wogan told to Major Gaydon at Strasbourg. Most men of Gaydon's age and weight would have shrunk from such an escapade. But Wogan knew his uncle. In a moment he was enlisted as one of the party. They also secured the services of Ensign Lucius O'Toole, and of Captain John Misset, who was not only a useful man in an emergency, but happened to possess a clever little Irish wife and—what was even more important—an equally clever little Irish-French maid. The wife was to be the Princess's companion; the maid, Jenny, was to enter the palace and change clothes with her. There was the difficulty that Mrs Misset was expecting a baby, being already four months gone; but no one seemed to bother much about that. Wogan bought a berlin and horses, with double sets of harness in case of accidents, and a supply of ropes. They secured passports in the names of the Count and Countess Cernes; Gaydon, as the most dignified figure among them, masqueraded as the Count, and Mrs Misset as the Countess, while Wogan figured on the passport as the Countess's brother and Jenny as her sister. These four (Jenny to be replaced later by the Princess) travelled in the berlin. O'Toole and Misset rode behind, temporarily assuming the character of servants. And there was also a real servant—one Michel, of the Pretender's household, of whom we shall presently have more to say.

There were one or two delays at the start of this amazing adventure. First there was a widespread rumour that James III had left Rome with the intention of proceeding in person to Innsbruck to rescue his Princess—in consequence of which the guards round the palace were doubled. Wogan tells an unlikely story to the effect that his own name was mentioned in this connexion, and that Gaydon became panic-stricken upon hearing of it. But then it appeared that James had spread this

rumour himself to throw spies off his track, he having in
fact departed on a political mission to Spain; and Chateaudoux wrote to Wogan that the guardianship of the
Princesses had now become slacker than ever. So the
rescue party had started off at last (the 17th of April)
unostentatiously (for it was thought undesirable to let
Colonel Dillon know of their intentions) but full of
courage; they had safely crossed the frontier, and had
sent Misset and Michel ahead of them with letters to
Chateaudoux and Clementina and instructions to proceed,
after delivering their letters, to the first village on the
line of retreat to Italy and there prepare relays of horses
against the arrival of the Princess and her rescuers.

And here was the main body, in Innsbruck at last,
tired and dishevelled, waiting for the return of Wogan,
who had gone out in the rain to meet Chateaudoux at
the trysting-place by the bridge. Why had not Chateaudoux sent to meet them as arranged? Whose was that
mysterious cloaked figure[1] that had followed their coach
all through the streets to the Black Eagle Inn? What
was this they heard about the Princess of Baden having
entered the town just before them? Why had she come
to Innsbruck? She would certainly be hostile to their
design if she knew of it. But for this infernal weather,
they might have travelled hither by night; but the roads
were mere quagmires, and they had been compelled to
expose themselves in broad daylight to all and sundry.
If they were recognized and arrested this side of the
frontier it would mean prison—if not the scaffold.
Quite apart from that, there was trouble waiting for the
Irish officers when they got back to France, if their
exploit was noised abroad. For Louis XV, knowing the
character of these Hibernian followers of his, and having
no desire to see Dillon's regiment denuded of officers,

[1] This mystery was never solved.

had announced his intention of immediately cashiering anyone engaging in unauthorized adventures, especially those of a character likely to annoy the rulers of friendly states. Gaydon and O'Toole remembered the parting words of the Governor of Strasbourg, a friendly soul, who was not supposed to have any official knowledge of their movements. "*Adieu, mes enfants*," he had said, "you are not crossing the Rhine for nothing: you seem to be engaged in an attempt to make a hole in the moon." A mad adventure indeed!

But I have drawn too gloomy a picture. When you get a group of Irish people at an inn it is a safe guess that the proceedings will be both humorous and lively. On this occasion the comic relief was provided by the ladies, Mrs Misset and Jenny—the first of whom was feeling far from well, while the second was in her tantrums. Jenny, it should be understood, had never been told the whole truth. She had been assured by Wogan and Misset that nothing more treasonable was intended than the rescue of a rich heiress, who was detained in this palace against her will by an envious relative. A girl of "sprightly and comical disposition," as all the authorities are agreed, she had readily consented to this proposal, and was, at the moment of our introduction to her, dividing her attention between reviving the fainting Mrs Misset and giving the two men a bit of her mind.

It is probable that her suspicions had been aroused, that she had begun to realize that the heroine of this adventure could be no ordinary heiress and that the result of failure might be extremely unpleasant to herself. But when they showed her the disguise she was expected to wear in the character of Chateaudoux's light o' love, and especially when she saw the low-heeled shoes that were to bring her height down to that of the Princess Clementina—she who was so proud of being tall and in her high heels could look straight into the blue eyes of her handsome friend O'Toole—then she quite definitely and literally 'kicked.' When the shoemaker attempted to try on those low-heeled monstrosities a shapely stockinged leg shot out at him, caught him square on the chest, and sent him sprawling. At last she put them on, but Jenny was angry and did not hesitate to say so. They had bribed her with money and clothes, but—well, everybody knew that she had only gone into this adventure for the sake of the Irish eyes of Lucius O'Toole; and there he was, the great oaf, whispering behind his hand to Major Gaydon and taking no more notice of Jenny than if she had never been born.

The big man may have heard more of her grumbling than she supposed. He has been described, not inaptly, as the Porthos of the party, but actually he had more wit than Misset or Gaydon, and he was the only one of them all who spoke German (though, of course, they all used French almost as their native tongue), and German was the language of Innsbruck. In fact, no buffoon, but the most practically useful of the Three Musketeers; in wit and initiative ranking only second to the leader.

But where was D'Artagnan? Listen! There is his step at last. The door swings open, and Wogan swaggers in, boastful, triumphant, the light of battle in his eyes, shaking the rain from his shoulders like a great spaniel dog. Chateaudoux, he explained, had been one whole hour late for the appointment; but he had come at last, and everything was arranged. He himself was to start for the palace forthwith, taking Jenny in tow (she tossed her head at this), but there was just time for a mouthful of food. He seated himself impetuously at the table. What he found there I do not know, except that it was not cold chicken, for it happened that the only provisions these feckless adventurers carried with them were certain

18

alleged chickens, which Wogan, at their last stopping-place, had roasted with his own hands, but which now turned out to be ancient hens, their flesh black and hard as leather. As he ate he glanced at Jenny and then at O'Toole lounging by the fire, then at Jenny again, appraising the situation.

Ten minutes later he was out in the street with her, struggling through the mud and the rain towards the palace gates. Then did Jenny uplift her voice in good earnest. She had inherited a fine flow of language from her mother, who was a French *vivandière*. Why, she asked, must she wear these frightful shoes? All the rest of the party went gaily dressed. What had she done wrong? She understood that she was to get into some one's bed, after changing clothes with her, and lie there for a while to avert suspicion. What harm in that? It wasn't a man's bed, was it? Why could not O'Toole, the big blackguard, do his own business? A plague on the whole lot of them! In her excitement she slipped and would have fallen in the mud, but Wogan caught her, raised her gently, and with many smooth and flattering speeches got her at last to the palace gate.

The luck was with him. The single sentry had taken refuge from the rain in one of the adjoining houses. Chateaudoux was waiting at the gate, and, while Wogan retired down the street, he escorted Jenny upstairs.

The little Princess had retired to bed early; but after waiting till the house was quite still she had risen again, and made hurried preparations for her flight. There was a letter of apology to be written to her mother, the Princess Sobieski (who probably knew all about it, but needed this document as some protection against the Emperor's wrath). There were her clothes to be packed, and her jewel-case. She darted about the room, full of the mad excitement of the occasion, divided between laughter and tears. At last everything was ready. A short pause and there came a knock at the door. There entered Chateaudoux, the gentleman-usher, and a cross-looking Irish girl.

There was no need for explanations. Jenny and the Princess rapidly changed clothes. But somehow the sight of that frowning face, on such an occasion, was too much for poor Clementina's nerves. She wept silently. Whereupon Jenny, instantly relenting, began to soothe and flatter her. "Madam, you little think how many you have made languish with an impatient desire to see you." And "I cannot but say you are very handsome, and richly worth the pains they have taken about you." And so she coaxed her back to smiles and her habitual good temper, and saw her give her hand confidingly to Chateaudoux and depart on her great adventure.

Clementina has been described by one who knew her at this time as "not a sparkling beauty," but " infinitely charming" and of "a wonderful quick comprehension." Wogan himself wrote of her, after their first meeting, that she had "the agreeableness of seventeen and the solidity of thirty"—a clumsy kind of compliment, but, like many Irishmen, he talked better than he wrote. A year or two after this an English Whig, the Marquis of Blandford, seeing her in Rome, felt compelled to acknowledge her "wit, vivacity, and mildness of temper," adding that she was "of middling stature, well-shaped, and has lovely features." What none of them sufficiently emphasizes are the courage and the delightful girlish sense of humour which stand out in every line of Wogan's and Gaydon's narratives. In fact, this girl, who was to be the mother of Bonnie Prince Charlie, would have made a charming Queen of England; and I cannot help thinking that if another English Whig, Horace Walpole, had chanced to know her at this time, instead of in her sad middle age, he would have sighed a little and shrugged his shoulders to think of the German Queen and the stout German *fraus* waddling along the path that was named after them at Hampton Court.

So Chateaudoux led her downstairs, across the court-yard, and to the outer gate, and there the gentleman-usher bade her farewell in a loud, hearty, and familiar voice (for the benefit of the porters). The soldier sentry was still absent, warming himself by some friendly fire. There was no reason for delay. The little Princess drew her cloak about her, and stepped out boldly into the darkness and the rain. But she had not stumbled many yards before a tall figure emerged from one of the door-ways and advanced to meet her. Charles Wogan! She knew him at once. Had they not been the best of friends at her father's Court in Silesia when he was acting Cupid's messenger? What exactly was the relationship between these two people history does not relate. Mr A. E. W. Mason has made a charming romance of it, and perhaps he is right. What is certain is that the Princess liked to chaff her cavalier, and that Wogan, usually so ready with his tongue, would be strangely confused and stammering in his replies to her.

She clinging to his arm, they hastened towards the Black Eagle through the muddy, rain-swept streets. Suddenly they encountered a filthy kennel, right across their path. How to get over it? To throw down your cloak, in the manner of Sir Walter Raleigh, upon that dirty running water would be—simply to lose a cloak. Peering down, he saw something white and, taking it for a large, flat stone, told her to step upon it. She did so, and was immediately over her ankles in water, for the stone was but a handful of straw! Poor Wogan, covered with shame, managed to get her out and to the farther shore, humbly apologizing and inwardly cursing himself.

But the Princess only laughed. The adventure was becoming more amusing every minute. She took his arm again, and they hurried on, heads bowed against the storm, and so came at last to the Black Eagle, where their friends were awaiting them, and where the berlin was already drawn up in the yard.

But what a scene when Mrs Misset beheld this bedraggled Princess! What cries of dismay! What reproaches! The Princess only laughed the louder and looked at Wogan where he stood abashed. Dry stockings were quickly found, but the poor child's limbs were almost frozen stiff, and if she were put into the coach for a long journey Mrs Misset would not answer for the consequences. Then some one had a happy thought—the gentlemen's muffs! In a moment the Princess's legs were put into them, and she herself into the coach; the horses were whipped up, the berlin clattered out of the inn yard. In this strange fashion did the Pretender's bride set out to meet him in Rome.

O'Toole, as knowing the language, had been left behind to settle with the landlord. When he overtook the berlin, some miles down the road, he found its occupants in a state of consternation. Clementina had just discovered that her jewel-case was left behind. So O'Toole swung his horse round and galloped back to Innsbruck. The streets were empty; evidently there had been no alarm. He entered the inn unperceived, and made his way upstairs to the room where the Princess had changed her stockings. He found the door fastened. He did not wish to call the landlord, for the sight of such a jewel-case as this would certainly have aroused curiosity. He therefore leaned his great weight against the door until the latch gave way. He saw an empty room, and the jewel-case on the table, just as Clementina had left it. Seizing it, he hastened downstairs, threw himself on his horse, and urged the animal once more down the southern road that led to Italy and safety.

Nor could any of these Irishmen yet feel their heads quite secure upon their shoulders—not even when they got to Brenner, their first stop, and found Misset and Michel waiting for them with a change of horses. This posting-station stood at the very top of the Brenner Pass, and the sun was just rising in the valley below them when they started again, bumping and jolting downwards over the muddy roads. O'Toole, Misset, and Michel were on horseback. Of those in the coach the 'Count' and 'Countess' of Cernes (Gaydon and Mrs Misset) probably slept. Clementina and Wogan talked. He told her of his adventures, his escape from Newgate, his campaigns in France. She inquired eagerly about England (the country she was never to see), and he taught her a few words of the English language. But they must have slept occasionally; for it is recorded that Wogan, who was hugging the precious jewel-case to his breast, dozed off and dropped it—and where should it fall but upon the head of Princess Clementina, who had collapsed, sound asleep, across his knees!

The rain had ceased, and the weather as they descended became noticeably warmer. The road at this point ran along the mountain-side, high above the banks of the rushing Adige. Wogan, to encourage the coachman and postilion to greater exertions, had supplied them with refreshments on so generous a scale that they were now, most unfortunately, drunk. Descending at a reckless speed towards a sharp bend in the road, they suddenly encountered a country cart, and, the coachman trying to avoid a collision, the coach tilted dangerously over the precipice—and must, indeed, have gone altogether had not one of the wheels been arrested against the stump of a tree, righting the vehicle just in time and enabling the horses to pull it clear. O'Toole, who was close behind and realized the peril they had been through more clearly than the ' insides,' came up in a blazing rage and laid on to the coachman and postilion with a whip. He believed, he said afterwards, that but for the presence of the Princess he would have killed them. Soon after this it was decided to leave O'Toole and Misset behind to act as a kind of rearguard to give warning of any signs of pursuit, and if possible to intercept the pursuers.

As their journey continued southward across the Austrian Tyrol, they became aware of an increasing difficulty in obtaining relays of horses; for it appeared that the ubiquitous Princess of Baden was once more travelling just ahead of them with a large suite, and was not only causing them acute anxiety, but was leaving all the inns horseless behind her as she went. At Trent, about ninety miles south of Innsbruck, the situation became acute. They dared not linger in this large town for fear of being recognized. Clementina was feverishly anxious to get on. She kicked off the men's muffs, for it was now intolerably hot, threw aside the furred hood which she had worn all the way, and even asked for a glass of wine and a biscuit, having hitherto refused any kind of refreshment but eggs.

But there was nothing much the matter with her nerves, as she presently showed. As they drove through Roveredo Wogan and Gaydon turned to the Princess and began to congratulate her upon having safely passed the last town with a military garrison in the Emperor's dominions. She laughingly warned them not to rejoice too soon. A minute later, as if her words had been prophetic, there was a loud crash, the coach lurched and stopped dead in the mud with a broken axle-tree. Clementina remained perfectly cool. Her only concern

CLEMENTINA SOBIESKI
Scottish National Portrait Gallery
Photo Annan, Glasgow   24

was for poor Mrs Misset, who was in no condition to endure such shocks.

They clambered out and looked around them. There was a pretty little Tyrolese village a few hundred yards away across the fields, and thither the Princess was escorted. Here she was given refreshments in one of the cottages; and two sturdy villagers were found who agreed, for a consideration, to walk on either side of the coach and hold up the roughly mended axle-tree. At no time during the journey had their prospects seemed so gloomy. They had still to cover forty miles to the frontier. Even if the coach held together it was becoming harder to find horses at every stop. Long before this the hue and cry must have started behind them, yet they had no news at all from Misset and O'Toole. "But the Princess was as gay and cheerful as if no disaster had, or was likely to, happen, and spirited up the others by her discourse and example." And after they had climbed back, carefully and gingerly, into the damaged coach, and had begun bumping slowly along the road again, she put her head back on a cushion and "slept very soundly." When presently the axle-tree broke again she did not even wake. But as they lifted her gently from the carriage her feet were accidentally splashed in a pool of water, and the cold waked her up. "What say you to this, Wogan?" she laughed. "You who always find stepping-stones to wet me!" And she shamed him still further by adding maliciously that she had been sleeping particularly well.

They patched the axle somehow, and the coach staggered on again. It was about this time that the servant Michel, in the absence of O'Toole, became the practical member of the party, and took the lead in finding and hiring horses. Once he saved the situation by producing two wretched old screws which, five minutes before, had been pulling a plough. A remarkable fellow was Michel, and an expert in escaping like Wogan himself. Every one knows how, after the failure of the Fifteen, when the Jacobite lords were in Newgate awaiting their execution, which was fixed for the following day, the wife of Lord Nithsdale, with a cool courage and devotion perhaps unequalled in the history of escapes, had managed to change clothes with her husband and get him smuggled out of the prison. What is not so generally known is the subsequent story of his escape to France. Lady Nithsdale herself has described it in a letter to Lady Lucy Herbert. They hid him first, she says, in the house of the Venetian Ambassador, but she dared not tell the Ambassador what she had done.

> But one of his [the Ambassador's] servants concealed him in his own room till Wednesday, on which day the Ambassador's coach-and-six was to go down to Dover to meet his brother. My lord put on a livery and went down in the retinue without the least suspicion, to Dover, where Mr Michel (which was the name of the Ambassador's servant), hired a small vessel and immediately set sail for Calais. The passage was so remarkably short that the captain threw out this reflection, that the wind could not have served better if his passengers had been flying for their lives, little thinking it to be really the case. Mr Michel might have easily returned without suspicion of having been concerned in my lord's escape; but my lord seemed inclined to have him with him, which he did, and he has at present a good place under our young master [the Old Pretender].

This Michel, then, was the same sturdy fellow who was now proving so useful in another historic escape. Strange how these obscure names will flash suddenly across a page or two of history! It must have been nervous work when, after the second breakdown of the axle-tree, they struggled into the next town and found, as usual, no horses. Michel pleaded with the coachman from

Trent to let his team go on another stage, drawing a light cart, while the coach was left behind to be repaired; whereupon the fellow asked, with a surly, suspicious air, "why they should hurry ladies on at such a rate."

Wogan bribed him into silence and acquiescence. The light cart was brought out. In jumped the Princess, followed more slowly by Mrs Misset. The men were to follow on foot. The last lap of the journey had begun. Again Clementina slept, and they had not the heart to wake her, until the absurd country cart clattered over the frontier and she opened her eyes to see smiling faces all round her and knew that she was in Italy, safe at last.

Then came Wogan and Gaydon, hot and dusty from their walk, and Misset and O'Toole with exciting news to tell. For it appeared that the Emperor had sent a courier after the fugitives with instructions to the frontier posts to intercept them at all costs. But O'Toole had spotted the man as he rode into the yard of the inn where Misset and he were seated at dinner, and had got him alone in the parlour and plied him with wine (surreptitiously laced with brandy by Misset). He had victoriously drunk him under the table, taken the despatches from him and destroyed them, put the poor man comfortably to bed, and ridden off with Misset to overtake their companions.

So there was a great forgathering and much rejoicing and mutual congratulation. But at the first village they came to on the Italian side Clementina insisted upon stopping the cart and getting out and finding her way to the village church. For Clementina was a strict Catholic —a fact not fully appreciated at the time.

There is only one thing lacking in this romantic story —the lover. That dull, industrious person was unable to attend at the frontier; he was busy with his politics in Spain. The marriage was to be performed by proxy.

Jenny deserves a footnote. All that night, after the departure of Clementina, the poor child lay quaking in the Princess's bed. On the following day Princess Sobieski *mère* was able to avert the usual morning inspection by asserting that her daughter was ill. But as the day wore on the good-natured old lady became anxious on Jenny's account in case a discovery should take place. As Wogan himself says—he who always swore to her that there was no sort of danger—"she might have paid with her life for her presence there, and who knows what transports of fury on the part of these barbarians she might have been subjected to?" Sobieski *mère* hustled the girl out of bed, and put her into a nasty little cubbyhole, where all the dirt and slops of the house were thrown. Jenny, not yet fully realizing her danger, violently resented this treatment, and afterwards declared that if there had been a window she would have flung herself out. But it saved her life, because suspicion had been aroused in some way, and the Governor made his evening inspection unexpectedly early.

When the Princess's absence was discovered there was a scene. The elder Princess, to save herself from further indignities, produced her daughter's letter, and then very wisely fainted right away. The only casualty was an unfortunate page, who, being suspected of some share in the escape, was chased and manhandled, and finally fell on his sword at the feet of the Princess Sobieski, but happily pinked no vital part. Many hours later, when the excitement had died down, a distinctly cross and rumpled Jenny was released from her malodorous cell. Let us hope that she was rewarded suitably. All that is known is that, the Princess Sobieski's sister, the Duchess of Parma, happening to arrive in Innsbruck in the midst of all this excitement, Jenny was smuggled out of the town as one of her attendants. She subsequently re-entered the service of the Missets, and died in that service in 1739.

Such were the romantic beginnings of poor little Clementina's married life. The ogre's castle, the rescue party, the flight through the darkness clinging to her cavalier, the headlong ride to the frontier, and her royal lover's waiting arms—it promised well. What maiden could desire more? Alas! she was to suffer many years of bitter disillusionment and to die without her reward. Yet the gods of romance and adventure do not in the end betray the faithful servants who put their lives in their hands. It would be a warped and sour judgment indeed which did not admit that, after all, the results of this rather famous marriage alliance more than justified its gay beginning.

CHAPTER II

"A KING WITHOUT A COUNTRY"

Bonnie Prince Charlie's father and mother were married by proxy at Bologna on the 9th of May, 1719, only a few days after the events recorded in the last chapter. The romantic party whom we left near the frontier resting themselves—for the ladies must have been nearly shaken to pieces in that country cart, Gaydon had hurt his foot against a rock while walking behind, and Wogan, Misset, and O'Toole were desperately short of sleep— had come limping into Bologna on the 2nd of May, and, after some hesitation, had taken rooms at the Pilgrim's Inn. But things were not very pleasant there. By some ironical jest of fate the inn happened to be full of English gentlemen—travellers returning homeward from a visit to Rome, and no doubt in a somewhat uproarious, holiday-making mood and displaying all that delicate consideration for the feelings of the natives for which our fellow-countrymen are still unfortunately famous abroad. Anyhow, they took an embarrassing interest in the fair Clementina, drinking no other health at their dinner-table, seizing every excuse to enter the room where she was, and little dreaming, of course, that the object of their admiration was the Pretender's bride.

Quite apart from these jovial fox-hunters, Clementina was attracting altogether too much attention at Bologna. For, in addition to her pretty face, she carried an air of distinction which could not be missed. People began to wonder who she was; there was gossip at the street-corners. So Wogan went to see the Cardinal Origo and told him all about it; and the Cardinal was, of course, delighted with his story, and immediately sent off messengers to Rome, and lent the Princess a house to live in with her followers until James's representatives arrived. The secretary, Murray, and his sister, Mrs Hay, reached Bologna from Rome on the 8th of May, and the marriage by proxy took place on the following day. Thereafter there was a royal progress to Rome in amusing contrast to that delightful, undignified scuttle from Innsbruck. And when Clementina entered the Eternal City on the 15th her cup of happiness must have been brimming full; for the Pope received her like a "regular royal Queen," royal honours were accorded to her everywhere, the crowds shouted themselves hoarse with enthusiasm as she passed through the streets to the palace which the Pope had lent her, and all Roman society was at her feet.

Clementina waited in Rome for her bridegroom more than three months. James was in Spain, but all his schemes had failed—gone off at half-cock. A small Irish-Spanish force had landed in the north of Scotland, Lucan was in Connaught; but the great Spanish armada, commanded by Ormonde, which was to have been directed against Bristol, where there were many Jacobite sympathizers, had been scattered by a storm (like its even greater predecessor) and had been forced to put back into port. James, hastening to join his supporters, had reached Corunna on the 17th of April, just as the fatal news arrived of the dispersal of the fleet. It must have been a bitter disappointment to him. There was no doubt at all about his personal gallantry. As a youngster in exile he had fought on the French side at Oudenarde, Lille, and Malplaquet, and had so distinguished himself that his name was known in both armies, and even the British soldiers are said to have cheered him and drunk his health when he rode out boldly to visit them in their outposts.

But that was long ago.   In the Fifteen he had shown that he lacked all the gifts of leadership—all the dash and imagination and personal magnetism which his son was to display in such generous measure when it was too late. He was one of the dull Jameses—honest, pedantic, industrious, no more.   It is a curious fact in the history of the association of the Stuarts with the throne of England that every one of them who was named James was of this uninspiring type, and every one who was named Charles was of an outstanding and attractive personality, with a power of winning the devotion of his followers perhaps unequalled in the annals of kingship. The Jameses lost the throne of England, the Charleses established a tradition of loyalty to it which is still a living force to-day.   Charles I was the Royal Martyr, the "White King"; Charles II made his people laugh in his lifetime (when they badly needed a laugh) and weep at his death; Charles Edward was—well, Bonnie Prince Charlie!

But the unfortunate James III, sitting up half the night in his private cabinet in the houses that people lent him to live in at Vincennes, Corunna, and Rome, scribbling out that endless correspondence of his, appealing for political and financial support to all who would listen, reminds us irresistibly of his unpleasant great-grandfather, with his long, lugubrious disquisitions on subjects he did not understand (the diatribe against tobacco is in a higher class), or his solemn, dignified father, striving, pen in hand, to save the soul of England against her will.

However, he had to get back to his bride some time, and when it became apparent that there was nothing further to be done in Spain he started homeward and met Clementina on the road somewhere near Montefias-cone on the 28th of August, 1719.   Clementina had her old friends of the rescue party with her, and when James had greeted her with all lover-like courtesy he turned to Wogan, and, according to that not too reliable historian, made the following handsome speech: "Wogan, you have comported yourself as I expected you would; and if I hope one day to ascend the throne which is mine by right it is in order, in some part, to repay you for all you have done for me." Wogan was created a baronet; Misset, Gaydon, and O'Toole were knighted, while the stout major was promoted to the rank (on paper) of brigadier in the English Army, the other two to be colonels. And here we may pause to note that Gaydon eventually died a lieutenant-colonel in the French service in about the year 1745, being then a very old man. O'Toole, while still a captain, was killed in action, fighting for France against the Emperor on the Moselle. Wogan and Misset went to Spain, and both rose to high rank. Of the former we shall have more to say presently. Misset died as Governor of Oran, in Barbary, in 1733, and Mrs Misset then retired to Barcelona and lived there quietly with the faithful Jenny.

James and Clementina were married again, and in person, at Montefiascone, Wogan being one of the witnesses, and then travelled together to Rome, where the Pope received them honourably, and gave them the Muti Palace to live in; and they settled down to that long period of sham royalty, empty pomp, and frustrated hopes which must surely have been as severe a test as any marriage alliance could be subjected to. And there, on New Year's Eve 1720, Prince Charles Edward Louis Philip Casimir, the Young Pretender, was born.

It was an event which stirred all the civilized world, and it gave rise to almost as many Whig lies as the birth of James III himself, who was alleged to have been smuggled into St James's Palace in a warming-pan. For the English Whigs were the first political party in Europe to study the art of propaganda. Our chief authority is Walton, the English agent at Rome, whose many letters to the Secretary of State in London describing events at the Muti Palace are preserved among the State Papers in the Public Record Office. They provide a unique instance of State Papers which are as unreliable for historical evidence as the backstairs gossip of a nursemaid.

Walton, in fact, had half the Pretender's servants in his pay, and he was careful to pass on only such titbits of news as he thought would please the authorities at home. He wrote of the infant Prince that "his legs are so turned inwards and distorted that it is very much in doubt if he will ever be able to walk." And, again, that his health "is such that every day reveals new imperfections in it, and consequently he will not live very long." At the same time another English Whig, the Marquis of Blandford, was describing him, in a letter to a friend, as "a fine, promising child." "The Prince is the finest child in the world," wrote Hay, a member of James's household, a year or two later, "healthy and strong, and runs about from morning till night." And we have the naïve self-revelation in Prince Charles's first letter, addressed to his father at the age of seven:

> DEAR PAPA,
> I thank you mightily for your kind letter. I shall strive to obey you in all things. I will be very dutifull to Mama, and not jump too near her. I shall be much obliged to the Cardinal for his animals. I long to see you soon and in good health.
> I am, dear Papa,
> Your most dutifull and affectionate son,
> CHARLES P.

In fact, so far from being the weakling pictured by Walton, he was from the outset a sturdy little boy whose leading

PRINCE CHARLES AS A BOY
A. David (?)
National Portrait Gallery   34

characteristics were an abounding vitality and a passion for outdoor sports. At the age of six he could ride and shoot; he would knock birds off the roof with a crossbow and "split a rolling ball with a bolt three times in succession." A few years later he had carried his passion for shooting so far that he would stay out long after dark with a shot-gun, trying to hit bats on the wing! He was also very fond of "the golf."

As to his personal appearance, most authorities are agreed in describing him as a "pretty, brown-eyed boy," though there was an English lady who saw him in Rome and maintained that his eyes were blue. But there is no problem of history more baffling to the biographer than this question of colour. Authorities are exasperatingly vague about it: they seldom mention the colour of a flag, of a ship's sides, of a man's hair—of his eyes least of all. Only recently there has been a fierce argument among historians as to the colour of the eyes of the beautiful Mary Queen of Scots, a point on which it seems preposterous that her contemporaries should have left us in any doubt. Bonnie Prince Charlie's physical charm arose not so much from the regularity of his features—which were comely, but not strikingly handsome—as from his large and beautiful eyes, which, if we may judge from his portrait, animated the whole face. It was a legacy from his mother, if she left him little else of value.

For the rest, most of his portraits show him rather plump in the face, and apparently with no chin to spare; but Horace Mann, one of the English agents in Italy, speaks of his "pointed" chin, and adds that he was "very thin" (probably from worry, for this was just before the Forty-five), and at least one of the existing likenesses bears this description out. Of his athletic build and natural grace of movement as he grew to manhood there seems to be no doubt. Friend and foe alike are agreed that he had personality—that he was, as the saying goes, every inch a king.

It is commonly accepted that the education of the child was deficient; but the evidence for this seems to rest almost entirely upon a weakness in spelling, which was not unusual in the early eighteenth century, and may sometimes be observed among schoolboys even to-day. Young Charles wrote "umer" for "humour," "sord" for "sword," and "Gems" for "James"—his own father's name! On the other hand, he displayed a marked aptitude for languages, and though his tastes were definitely not literary, no one associated with his upbringing seems to have thought him stupid. The real trouble about his education was not one of spelling, but, as we shall see, of religion.

He was growing up into rather a spoiled but lovable boy, and we soon begin to hear of his having "got out of the hands of his governors." James had not been particularly lucky in his choice of tutors for his son. The first, James Murray, never got on with the boy, who first disliked and then despised him. On one occasion young Charles disgraced himself by threatening to kick or, alternatively, to kill his tutor. For this they locked him in his room, and as he was already an efficient shot at the age of six they were careful to put all firearms out of his reach. Ewald[1] has well pointed out that this violence was entirely alien to Charles's real character, for as he grew to manhood he showed himself humane and considerate to the last degree. One or two attempts were made to introduce the Chevalier Ramsay in Murray's place; but Ramsay could not endure the atmosphere of intrigue and discontent at the Pretender's Court, though he was attracted by his young pupil almost against his will. "He is continually in motion," he says; and adds

[1] A. C. Ewald, *The Life and Times of Prince Charles Stuart*, vol i, p. 42 (1875).

an interesting comment on Walton's gossip: "No porter's child in the country has stronger legs and arms."

In the meantime poor Clementina's life romance was not working out very well. James was temperamentally unsuited to the part she had cast him for as she sat dreaming in her palace prison at Innsbruck. He was always busy and always hard up, so that he often found it difficult to raise the money for his footmen's wages; and as the years slipped by it seemed less and less likely that she would ever experience the sensation of sitting beside him enthroned in Westminster Abbey. James had a distaste for society, a deplorable trait in the husband of a young and pretty wife. Moreover, Clementina disliked those immediately about him, people whom she was compelled to see every day. These were Colonel John Hay (created Earl of Inverness by James) and his wife (of whom Clementina was desperately jealous) and the tutor, James Murray (whom she disliked first for his own sake, and secondly because he was a Protestant). She had not been allowed to keep her friends, the Missets.

In truth the religious difficulty was at the root of the whole trouble, and it is extraordinary that neither the pious little maiden whom we met in the last chapter nor either of her parents should have foreseen it. That James himself was a good Catholic was enough for them. But now, when Clementina found a Church of England chaplain supported in the Muti Palace at James's expense, and conducting there daily services which were often attended by English visitors to Rome; and when she heard her husband, in such heretical company, enunciating those broad principles of toleration which he declared his intention of putting into force when he recovered his throne; and, above all, when she saw that her son was being deliberately instructed in a kind of mixture of the two religions, so that he might pass muster with either, and would certainly end by believing neither—then Clementina's deepest feelings were outraged, and she was soon in open opposition to James. In this she was, not unnaturally, encouraged by her ecclesiastical friends, though it is difficult to believe that even the least worldly of cardinals can have failed to see the obvious necessities of James's position. It was no more than an elementary stroke of policy to spread the impression at home that the education of the heir to the throne was in Protestant hands, and that in general he was to be no mincing foreigner but British to the core—as much so in his religion as in his passion for outdoor sports. James was anxious that he and his family should always be thought of as British exiles, not as half-foreign pretenders. There is an interesting letter from the Marquis of Blandford which bears upon this point of difference between James and his wife. Speaking of the daily life at the Muti Palace, he says:

> There is every day a regular table of ten or twelve covers well served, unto which some of the qualified persons of his Court or travellers are invited; it is supplied with English and French cookery, French and Italian wines, but I took notice that the Pretender ate only of the English dishes, and made his dinner of roast beef. . . . He also preferred our March beer (which he has from Leghorn) to the best port wine. He drinks his glass of champagne very heartily, and to do him justice, he is as free and cheerful at his table as any man I know; he spoke much in favour of our English ladies, and said he was persuaded he had not many enemies amongst them, and then he carried a health to them. The Princess, with a smiling countenance upon the matter, said, "I think then, Sir, it would be just that I drink to the cavaliers."

This policy was to a large extent successful, but it owed its success not so much to the personal exertions of James, whose histrionic gifts were negligible, as to the skilful exploitation of the attractive personalities of his two little sons (for Charles had now a younger brother). In May 1722 Walton had noted sneeringly that the Princess was going through a course of bathing in the waters of three fountains which were believed to have the property of "facilitating conception." In his opinion, and in that of various "ladies" whom he had consulted, "connoisseurs in the art of making children," the Princess was incapable of having another child. Less than three years later Prince Henry, Duke of York, was born—as healthy and handsome a child as Charles, but of a very different disposition, grave, studious, and gentle. The boys made a happy contrast, each of them delightful in his own way, and their father did not neglect to let them be seen in public, that their youthful charms might touch the hearts of English visitors. He forced himself to take them out and to give parties, which he disliked. In April 1730, when Charles would be ten and his brother five, Walton records a "large assembly" at which the elder Prince danced and the younger sang, to the admiration of all beholders. Walton says that the Jacobites had managed to noise it abroad that "it was not against any Act of Parliament" for English visitors to pay the Princes their respects. Consequently "this custom of doing homage to the two little boys gains ground every day among the young people travelling here, and is degenerating into a kind of tenderness and compassion for the two boys." Walton thinks it his duty to warn the Secretary of State that "this evil is making great progress here."

But long before this the quarrels between James and Clementina had come to a head, and had done such damage to the Jacobite cause that all the innocent diplomacy of the little Princes could hardly repair. Clementina's growing jealousy of Mrs Hay, and James's obstinate refusal to dismiss the lady, were the immediate cause of the catastrophe. What justification there was for these suspicions we do not know; no evidence that is worth anything has come down to us. There is little in James's past record to suggest that he would have flouted his wife in this fashion. On the other hand, Clementina had hated all these people from the start, and was no doubt ready to believe the worst of them. She felt herself humiliated every hour of the day. Yet she could do nothing to assert herself while she remained in the Muti Palace; the dignified, unbending personality of her husband overawed her; she bounced off him like an indiarubber ball.

So she opened communications with the authorities of a neighbouring convent, and one night slipped quietly away and took refuge there. James was bitterly enraged. He would not yield an inch. He even appeared at the opera with Mrs Hay—an idiotic gesture which at once convinced most people of his guilt. Yet, as Joseph Surface pointed out to Lady Teazle, it is often "the consciousness of your own innocence" that drives people into hasty acts of this kind.

Meanwhile Clementina, from her convent, was stating her case to the world. She wrote to the Pope and accused James not only of adultery (which might have been forgiven), but of bringing his sons up as heretics (which was not to be borne). Prince Charles when he was introduced to the Holy Father made an unexpectedly good showing with his Catechism, and did much to smooth matters out. But in the meantime his father was definitely under a cloud. The Pope wrote him a strong letter (and it must be remembered that the Pope was his paymaster); and Cardinal Alberoni, the ex-dictator of Spain, who had recently invited him to that country and done him many services, now called upon him and began to scold him like a naughty schoolboy. James lost all patience and told the Cardinal in so many words to mend his manners and mind his business.

At this the Cardinal, rising in such fury that his robes were torn by the arms of his chair, replied that he had never failed to speak the truth in the presence of powerful sovereigns, who could have had him executed on the spot, and much less was he to be intimidated by a King without a country.

And with that he strode off home to indite a long letter to James telling him exactly what he thought of him.[1] Alberoni had accepted every word of Clementina's story as she told it. So did most people. Lockhart, James's agent in Scotland, wrote to him that this business of Mrs Hay was "the severest stroke your affairs have got these many years." Lockhart himself swallowed Clementina's story whole; he spoke of Mrs Hay as "the coquette," and remained permanently prejudiced against the Hays, and against James personally, for the rest of his life. It is hardly too much to say that the Jacobite party was for the moment split in two on this issue—and it need not be added that most of the party sided with the romantic Princess of the Innsbruck adventure rather than her stiff and solemn husband. The Cause was done incalculable harm.

While Clementina was still entrenched in her convent James permitted her two little boys to see her. He had recently been annoyed by a message from the Pope referring to his "concubinage" with Mrs Hay, to which he had replied by threatening to throw the Pope's messenger out of the window—or so somebody told the English agent. There was a rumour that Prince Charles was being forced to recite the subversive line: "A fig for the priests, all monks are rascals, the Mass cost my grandfather three kingdoms." Yet James was

[1] State Papers, Italian States, November 22, 1725.

desperately anxious to come to terms with Clementina, if it could be done without yielding a point. She, on her part, had a portrait made of her two little sons, and hung it up in her lonely cell—a pathetic touch, which no doubt won her many new supporters. She was a better public controversialist than James, though she might not be his match across the breakfast-table.

In the end the obstinate man had to capitulate. He promised to dismiss the Hays and Murray, and so managed to inveigle Clementina back. A Mr Stafford was officially appointed tutor, though Murray still hung about. The Hays paid visits, and Clementina steeled herself to receive them graciously. Her romance was dead. The little Princess of Innsbruck was buried and forgotten; all that remained was a hard, embittered pietist, who thought the world well lost for a religious dogma, and was deliberately pursuing a course of conduct that every day made more unlikely the realization of her girlhood's dream of sitting on a royal throne.

Yet one of her visitors at the convent had been Wogan. We shall never know what passed at that last interview between the Chevalier and his Princess. Did they remember the handful of straw which he had mistaken for a stepping-stone? Or that new use for gentlemen's muffs? The only thing certain is that Wogan returned to Spain, and so distinguished himself that he was made a provincial governor. He wrote a number of rather solemn letters to his friend Dean Swift, in the course of which he expressed his contempt for a popular play of the period called *The Beggar's Opera*. He took no active part in the Forty-five.

In dreaming of his adventures when he grew to be a man, as small boys love to do, Prince Charles, we may safely guess, had always pictured himself as a soldier-king. No doubt he had seen visions of the storming of

HENRY, LATER CARDINAL YORK
J. M. Nattier (?)
National Portrait Gallery

42

London, himself leading his loyal followers into the breach, while the fat German usurper fled quaking through the opposite gate. It must have been obvious to those around him that this was the boy's natural aptitude. He would be a man of action or nothing.

Among the visitors to the Muti Palace in the summer of 1734 was the Duke of Liria, afterwards better known as the Duke of Berwick, himself a Stuart (for he was the son of James's natural brother) and already an enthusiastic soldier. The Duke was on his way to join the Spanish army under Don Carlos, then engaged in the successful campaign which gave Naples to the Spanish Bourbons. The year 1734 was a bad one for the Emperor; his enemies were attacking him on every side; and in Naples, a distant outpost of the Empire, there could be little hope of relief. The Imperialist garrison had thrown itself into the town of Gaëta, and was there holding out desperately against Don Carlos and his Spaniards. Liria talked eagerly of the prospects of the siege; the Austrians, though outnumbered, were good soldiers: it would not be so easy. Prince Charles, now nearly fourteen, sat listening with his eyes popping out. Liria, for his part, loved the boy, as most visitors did, and very soon he had got permission from James to take the heir along with him to the siege lines of Gaëta.

They had a journey of seventy-five miles southward, until they descended from the Volscian mountains towards the sea and saw at their feet the white tents of the besieging army and the semicircle of the earthworks; beyond that the walls and spires of Gaëta; and beyond that again the blue waters of the gulf to which the town gives its name. Suddenly Charles felt a singing in his heart. They could hardly hold him back. It chanced that on that very first day of their arrival (the 6th of August, 1734) Liria was ordered to the front-line trenches, and the Prince, of course, went with him. It was a rough baptism of fire for a boy of fourteen. "The bullets hissed about his ears," says Liria, but he "showed not the least concern." On the contrary, he was enjoying himself.

Liria was not quite so happy about it. In a letter written after the siege he confesses that the Prince made him "pass some uneasy moments." (We are reminded of the many uneasy moments passed by the staff officers who accompanied another English prince to the front-line trenches in our own time.) On the following day Liria was relieved from trench duty, and took the Prince back with him. But they discovered that the house allotted to them as billets was in a very much exposed position, and had already been shot through again and again with cannon-balls. Liria promptly moved his quarters; but he could not dissuade the Prince from going into the house and examining the shot-holes, though five Austrian pieces were playing on it at the time.

After six days Gaëta surrendered. Charles's first brief adventure was over. It only remained for him to accompany Don Carlos in the victorious march to Naples, and to ride into the city beside him through the cheering crowds. It is an ancient saying that you never know a man till you have fought beside him (or a woman till you have kissed her), and it is therefore interesting to note the impression which young Prince Charlie made upon his comrades-in-arms. He had won golden opinions everywhere. There can be very few cases in history of a boy of his age scoring such a personal triumph. "I am now," writes Liria, "blessed be God, rid of all my uneasiness, and joyfully indulge myself in the pleasure of seeing the Prince adored by officers and soldiers: his manner and conversation are really bewitching, and you may lay your account that were it otherwise I would not have kept it secret from you." There is a general chorus to the same effect in a collection of letters written from the camp at Gaëta, and now among the State papers at the Record Office— how he mixed freely with the soldiers, how he delighted them by speaking to each in his own language, French, Spanish, or Italian. "A young prince so affable and of so charming a behaviour," writes one of them, "cannot fail of being adored both by officers and men." "The prince exceeds anything I was capable of fancying about him," says another, "and meets here with as many admirers as he has spectators." They all concluded that he was "born to a happy fate, and to make others happy too." Alas!

The picture that we get of the Prince at this time (or during the next few years) is, indeed, entirely charming. He is no mere boor of an outdoor boy. To his natural affability he has added social gifts: he plays the violin "continually," and he dances almost as well as he shoots. The old records are full of his wonderful dancing, which was to flutter the hearts of the ladies of Scotland ten years hence. He is entirely without vices. Walton, who would accuse him of anything, said later that he had "a strong leaning to women." The charge is as false and silly as the Whig insinuations against his courage—silly because by attacking him at his strongest points they only discredit the whole of their case against him.

The notorious Duke of Wharton (who had every vice except disloyalty to the Stuart cause) upon hearing of the appointment of James Murray as Charles's tutor wrote: "Make my compliments to him, and desire him that he will not only train the Prince for glory, but likewise give him a polite taste for pleasurable vice." Thus the eighteenth century! As a matter of fact, Murray taught him no more vice than he taught him spelling. The young Prince attracted women strongly, but he was not attracted by them. Nor did he show any tendency to

over-indulgence in wine. Why should he ? He probably never gave a thought to these things. He was
just a magnificent young animal, warm-hearted, impulsive, popular, trained to the last degree of mental and
physical fitness, clean and taut and ready when the
opportunity came to make his spring.

CHAPTER III

THE SEVEN MEN OF MOIDART

THE return of the fourteen-year-old warrior from Gaëta was a joyous occasion. He had proved himself a man. He had shown the world that there was still a Stuart to be reckoned with. "Everybody," writes Walton, "says that he will be in time a far more dangerous enemy to the present establishment of the Government of England than ever his father was."

The King of Naples had quite lost his heart to him, and had presented him with two horses as well as a gift of jewellery. He had started the campaign with a supply of pocket money from his father, augmented by a handsome present from the Pope before starting south, and had, of course, drawn his pay as an officer while attached to the army. So that he must have returned home in September 1734 with full pockets and almost bursting with pride, feeling himself already a man of reputation and substance. Whether his tutors found him any more manageable is another question.

That was a happy autumn. But on the 18th of January, 1735, his mother died. Poor Clementina! Broken-spirited, disillusioned, sourly submissive, she hastened thus early from a world which had so sadly disappointed her girlhood's hope. An affectionate boy is likely to feel the loss of his mother at fourteen more severely than at any other period of his life. In spite of her ill-health and her rather oppressive piety in later years, Charles must have known how much he owed to Clementina, must have felt that there was something gone out of the world

47

which he had unconsciously drawn upon and relied on
and must now do without—something which had sweet-
ened his life and which he would never know again.

The next and most obvious move in the education of
the young Prince was a kind of 'grand tour' through
those parts of Southern Europe where political conditions
were such that he could be received with something
approaching royal honours. After a year at home in the
Muti Palace (a blank year about which we know almost
nothing) he set forth in May 1737 to visit the principal
cities of Northern Italy, with a possible glimpse of Spain
in the background. He travelled as the Duke of Albano,
from the little town of that name in the mountains south
of Rome where the Pretender and his family were in the
habit of spending the summer months. There was a
farewell interview with the Pope, who gave timely
financial assistance; and then begins a long series of letters
from Walton, the British agent, to the Secretary of
State, full of envious descriptions of the reception given
to the Prince at every succeeding town and of gloomy
prognostications as to the likely effects of the tour. At
Bologna and Parma there were military displays in his
honour, and towns which he had not yet reached, like
Venice, were feverishly preparing *fêtes* such as would only
be offered to a reigning prince. He is "the fashionable
idol at the moment." At Florence, whither Walton had
now retired (alleging that he was afraid of being assassi-
nated by the Jacobites if he remained in Rome), the
Court of Tuscany held back discreetly, but all the leading
Florentine families drove out in their carriages to meet
Prince Charles, gave balls and dinner-parties in his
honour, and quite discounted the official coldness. Visits
to Pisa, Leghorn, and Siena followed. English Whig
visitors were disgusted to observe the enthusiasm with
which the Pretender's son was everywhere received.

Accompanying the Prince were the unfortunate James Murray, who rode in the same chair with him and to whom he was evidently insufferably rude; Henry Goring, whom he also disliked; and Strickland, another tutor. He worried his father by his failure to write home. By the end of the summer he was back in Rome, and Walton is busily retailing rumours of contemplated marriage alliances, none of which came to anything. Charles was now eighteen.

He was keen to go on with his military training; and his proud and politic father was at least equally anxious that he should attain proficiency in this profession of his choice. But it appeared that there was no army in Europe in which he could be allowed to serve. France and Spain refused at once; he might be a brilliant young soldier for his age, but he could hardly be regarded as a make-weight against the enmity of England. He was not even allowed to join an expedition which the Emperor was preparing against the Turks. No one outside Italy would employ him. Even his Italian friends were beginning to feel the weight of King George's displeasure. When news reached London of the *fêtes* given to Charles at Venice the Venetian Ambassador at St James's was peremptorily dismissed.

So he resumed his shooting expeditions—there was nothing else to do. Andrew Lang has quoted [1] an interesting letter from Charles's father, dated the 1st of October, 1742, in which the young man is described as "quite wearied of this country" (all his thoughts being in those northern islands which he had not seen), and James adds: "I don't wonder at it, for his sole amusement here is to go out shooting, to which he has gone every other day during all this season before daybreak, whether fair or foul, and has killed a great deal of game, such as this

[1] *Prince Charles Edward Stuart*, pp. 52-53 (1903).

place affords." Mr Edgar, James's secretary, has recorded how Charles would often refuse to go to bed, preferring to doze in a chair, with his riding-coat thrown over him, all gartered and ready, so that he might be away with his gun at one or two o'clock in the morning. The servants who accompanied him on these expeditions would be completely exhausted, though specially selected for the service; but James proudly describes how his sturdy son upon returning home "sits down and diverts himself with music for an hour or two, as if he had not been abroad." Charles had music in his soul. His brother Henry had a better singing voice when he chose; but Charles "plays his part upon the bass viol extremely well, for he loves and understands musick to a great degree."

And so time passed on, shooting season succeeded shooting season, dance followed dance, and every new piece of music was eagerly sought for. Charles was now in his early twenties, tall and slim, in the first flush of his athletic young manhood and his extraordinary personal charm. And he had done almost nothing! "What a pleasure it would be," exclaimed Edgar in a letter to the Earl Marischal, "to see better game than the shooting of quails."

But while Charles was shooting quail the Scottish and English Jacobites had not been entirely idle. It is true that the latter had contributed little to the Cause except words. The futile and premature Atterbury conspiracy had failed, and Bishop Atterbury himself was a fugitive on the Continent. English Tories, though they rather enjoyed drinking to the King over the water, were reluctant to come out into the open or even to subscribe secretly to the Jacobite funds. They were much clearer about their hatred of Walpole than their love of the Old Pretender. Yet even the Whig leaders were not above hedging on the main issue. Walpole himself and the Duke of Argyle, the head of the Campbells and the chief supporter of King George in Scotland, had both of them at different times been in communication with James; and though they may have disclosed the correspondence to the King and won credit thereby, it seems likely that Walpole, at any rate, kept in view the value of such letters should the Stuarts ever return.

The Old Pretender was shrewd enough, and by this time disillusioned enough, to estimate such professions at their true worth. There is no evidence that he ever took Walpole's approaches seriously (no doubt he remembered the great Duke of Marlborough's letters to his exiled father). On hearing of the death of George I in 1727 he had hurried first to Nancy and afterwards to Avignon, hoping for an invitation from his supporters in England. But nothing had happened. The French Government tactfully hustled him back across the Italian frontier. He never crossed it again.

But though Walpole as Prime Minister was still an enemy, even bringing gifts, it was not so much his personal influence as the policy he represented which was fatal to the Jacobite Cause. The time had long passed (it passed in 1715) when James could usefully fish in any but troubled waters. So long as there was peace in Europe no Government would have anything to do with him. Even the Pope (who subsidized him) said that if the English Jacobites wanted another Restoration they must pay for it. But immediately any European Government found itself at war with England it began to make gestures of friendship towards James. And the next important thing that happened in England, from James's point of view, was that the rising disgust with Walpole's methods of government resulted at last in the rupture of that long European peace which it had been the main object of his foreign policy to perpetuate. Spain was pursuing her old dog-in-the-manger policy in the West; English merchant skippers and Spanish officials were always more or less in a state of war in American waters; and the sad story of Captain Jenkins, who was arrested and mutilated like a malefactor for some alleged illegality, at last led to an explosion of popular indignation in England which forced Walpole, much against his will, into a declaration of war (October 1739). Yet the War of Jenkins's Ear, as it was called, was of little use to James, mainly because of the extraordinary slackness with which it was prosecuted. The Spanish Government was as little enthusiastic in the matter as was Walpole himself; to have produced the Pretender would merely have been to exacerbate English public opinion and perhaps to galvanize the British Admiralty into effective action against the islands of the West Indies. James was not invited to repeat his earlier visit to Spain.

In Scotland, however, the Jacobite Cause was as vigorously alive as everywhere else it seemed to be dead. It is not easy to account for the burst of activity which began with the visit to Paris of John Gordon of Glenbucket in 1737. Its origins are, at any rate, somewhat outside the scope of this book. But Glenbucket and his successors in the business were adventurers of such strange and varied types, their motives often so obscure, their actions so inconsequent, their speeches so wild, that they would be worthy of study even if they had not been closely associated with the career of Prince Charles. Glenbucket was not a territorial chieftain in the Highlands, and such influence as he possessed with the clans was entirely due to his own personality. He had fought in the Fifteen, and when he arrived in Paris was already a man of sixty-three. Finding that he could get little out of the French Government, he went on to Rome, and so impressed James with his promises (for instance, he guaranteed the co-operation of his son-in-law, Glengarry) that the Pretender wrote to William Cecil, the Jacobite agent in London, in a tone of quite unjustifiable elation. Glenbucket was followed by Lord Sempill, who was more than half a Frenchman, and talked with cheerful optimism of the unpopularity of the English Whigs and the readiness of the Tories to rise in rebellion. In point of fact, Cecil and his friends had been horrified on hearing from James of these rosy prophecies. James and his advisers, mostly foreigners, "mistook the outcry of faction and party rage for the voice of disaffection and revolt," as the contemporary Whig historian, John Home, remarks.

In Scotland the Jacobite leaders had formed an Association, or "Concert," consisting of the Duke of Perth, Lord John Drummond, Lord Lovat, Lord Linton (afterwards Earl of Traquair), his brother, the Hon. John Stuart, Donald Cameron the younger, of Lochiel, and his father-in-law, Sir John Campbell of Auchenbreck. The secretary was William Macgregor (or Drummond) of Balhaldy. In December 1739 Balhaldy went to Rome as the representative of the Association; and he also, carried away no doubt by his ardour for the Cause, painted the situation in colours far too bright. James passed him on to Paris, and there he met Sempill, and the two of them opened up negotiations with Cardinal Fleury, the French Prime Minister.

This was about three months after the outbreak of the War of Jenkins's Ear, and the astute Fleury put them off by pointing out that France was still officially at peace with England, whereas Spain was openly at war. Should they not address themselves in the first instance to Madrid? They did, but were frostily received. Then there was a proposal to hire a Swedish army to invade

England in French and Jacobite pay. They were to sail from Holland. Unfortunately, some Amsterdam journalist got hold of the story and printed it in full in a local news-sheet, so that the scheme had to be abandoned forthwith. This must be one of the earliest-known examples of the disastrous results of a newspaper 'scoop'! Finally, Fleury offered Balhaldy all the Irish troops in the French service, with a money grant of £20,000. With this proposal in his pocket, Balhaldy returned to Scotland *via* London. In the English capital he had interviews with the Earls of Orrery and Barrymore, Sir Watkin Williams Wynn, and Sir John Hynde Cotton (the leading Jacobite member of the House of Commons). The Scottish Jacobites, though they were somewhat dashed by Fleury's refusal to send French regular troops, nevertheless accepted his offer with a good show of enthusiasm. They sent Balhaldy back with a cordial letter.

It is now that we hear for the first time of John Murray of Broughton (not to be confused with James Murray, the tutor), who was presently to succeed Urquhart as Jacobite agent in Scotland. Murray, an active and business-like person, attempted to start a subscription list in Scotland when he heard what the Association had done. But he never raised a penny, because every one was afraid to head the list. Nor would the Association permit him to set in motion any active propaganda. This John Murray was later to become infamous as "Mr Evidence Murray," who saved his own skin after the failure of the Forty-five by becoming the leading witness for the Crown against his former associates. At the moment, however, he was probably the most active and practical worker on the Jacobite side.

There was now a period of acute and nerve-racking suspense all over Europe, and not least in the little exiled

Court at Rome. The death of the Emperor Charles VI in 1740 had raised the whole question of the Austrian succession and gradually all the leading European states were becoming involved in war. It was obviously only a question of time before France and England should be drawn into the struggle on opposite sides. This would be the Jacobites' opportunity; this would be, in modern phraseology, *Der Tag*. They waited eagerly.

Early in 1742 Balhaldy arrived in Edinburgh from Paris, where the atmosphere had become noticeably more cordial. He brought with him a definite proposal from Fleury; which was to send over an army of 13,000 men, of whom 1500 were to be landed in the West Highlands of Scotland, and 1500 on the east coast and at Inverness, while the main body, consisting of 10,000 men commanded by Marshal Saxe, and having young Prince Charles on board with them, would steer for the Thames and land as near as possible to London. This was getting down to business at last!

But still nothing happened; another year drifted by; the English Government continued to stand aside from the European war. In January 1743 the Association determined to send Murray over to Paris to find out how the land lay. On his way he heard of the death of Fleury, and when he came to discuss matters with Amelot, the French Minister in charge of Foreign Affairs, it was only to be told that the King of France would do nothing until he had received an assurance of support from the English Jacobites when Marshal Saxe landed. "The French Government," wrote Walton sneeringly, "are using the Pretender and his followers like so many marionetts, making them dance to any tune which suits the interests of France." The Jacobites themselves were at sixes and sevens. The Earl Marischal, a cautious conservative person, talked to Murray and confirmed him in his distrust of those breezy optimists, Balhaldy and Sempill. The conspirators seldom opened their minds to each other frankly, but each man listened while the other talked, and then sent off private reports to Scotland and to Rome. "At the end of 1743," says Andrew Lang, "the Jacobite party was a mere chaos of suspicion and contradictory counsels."

In Rome James was playing a waiting game (which was the only kind of game open to him) with considerable skill and discretion. Himself he kept in the background; but he seized every opportunity of exploiting the popular personality of his elder son. His one idea, according to Walton, was to "get his elder son to appear on the European stage, for he is the idol of the whole Jacobite party." Charles himself must have been on tenterhooks. We may guess that much of that feverish energy which he threw into his shooting expeditions was the result of a condition of nervous excitement which might have told severely upon a less vigorous constitution than his.

At last the great day dawned. England and France had come to blows, and the first clash of arms at Dettingen, which set the church-bells ringing in London, was equally glorious news in Rome, especially for the young soldier who had been eating his heart out there for so long. King Louis was furious at the defeat, and the first symptom of his wrath was a sudden enthusiasm for the Jacobite Cause in startling contrast with his previous apathy. That George II should have been present in person at Dettingen and distinguished himself by a kind of clumsy heroism added bitterness to the pill. Fleury's plan was immediately set in motion: troops began to assemble at Dunkirk; Charles was summoned from Rome (January 1744).

It was given out that he was starting on one of those mad shooting expeditions in the middle of the night.

Leaving town with only a few companions, he galloped through the darkness in the direction of Albano, though his real destination was Genoa, in the north. It was then that the tutor, James Murray, was called upon to perform his last service to an ungrateful pupil. He had a convenient 'accident.' His horse upset him into a ditch. Charles went to his assistance, and while the rest of the party were thus got rid of they hurriedly changed clothes, and, making a wide *détour*, spurred hard for Genoa. It was an adventurous start to the great adventure, and highly characteristic of this Prince of Adventurers who never travelled anywhere in the ordinary humdrum way. At Genoa he took boat for the little port of Antibes, near Cannes, and arrived at Paris in the same month. He travelled so fast that the two or three servants with him almost collapsed, so that, as he wrote to his father, if the journey had been any longer "I should have been obliged to get them tyed behind the chaise with my portmantle, for they were quite *rendu*." From Paris he went to Gravelines and there remained *incognito*, waiting for the signal to join the French fleet at Dunkirk. In the meantime he had conferred with the leading Jacobites in the capital, including Sempill and Marischal, and had made the acquaintance of Lord Elcho, to whom we owe the best account of the events which immediately followed.

The Stuarts, on the whole, were good losers. Neither on the scaffold nor as hunted fugitives was it their habit to indulge in lamentations or complain that the dice had been loaded. Yet they had at least one legitimate grumble against fate—the luck of the weather seems almost always to have been against them. Marshal Saxe was at Dunkirk embarking his men. His transports were anchored out in the roads, so that the troops had to be conveyed in lighters, and progress was slow. However, they had got about ten thousand men on board, and the decks of the transports were bright with their blue uniforms; Saxe himself and Charles were ready to embark, when a storm of unprecedented fury arose and continued for many days, dispersing the French warships that had come from Brest to protect the embarkation, and driving the transports ashore with considerable loss of life. The delay was fatal. An English fleet had put to sea and was patrolling the Channel. Marshal Saxe was instructed from Paris to inform the Prince that the scheme was abandoned.

It might well have broken his heart. Yet, so far as can be seen, he never lost courage for a moment. He remained obstinately at Gravelines, constantly urging his principal adviser, the aged Earl Marischal, to importune the French Government to send out the Scottish expedition at least, even if the English scheme must be given up. He was told, "No." Then he asked if he might serve in the French Army, but again the answer was "No"—it would only annoy his supporters in England. In fact, the Earl Marischal appeared to be opposed to doing anything, and Charles wrote to Rome describing in a tone of humorous despair the boredom of reading and answering long letters advising caution—he says they were "rather books"—from this early advocate of the policy of "Wait and see." Privately he never wavered in his determination to renew the attempt—if not immediately, then in the following summer—whether the French backed him or not.

He removed from Gravelines to Montmartre, near Paris. His principal associates were now Sir Thomas Sheridan, a former tutor of his, who had been with him at Gaëta and of whom he was genuinely fond; George Kelly, also an Irishman, who had been Atterbury's secretary; and a certain Father Kelly, some relation of

George's, who was Charles's confessor, and was said to drink more than was good for him. These Irishmen quarrelled incessantly with Balhaldy and Sempill, the Scots. The Prince became to some extent involved in these quarrels; he was only a youngster, and it was inevitable that he should take sides. But though he had his likes and dislikes, and wrote one or two letters which brought from his father a very proper rebuke, it was remarkable how he never lost sight of the main object, how hard, clear, and logical was his thought (among all these irrelevant squabblers), how resolute and decisive his actions compared with those of either his father or his grandfather in the crises of their lives.

He seems to have been almost the only one among the Jacobites, whether in Scotland, England, or on the Continent, who perceived, as we perceive to-day, that it had become before everything else a question of time— that Queen Anne had been dead thirty years; that everywhere except in the Highlands the flame was flickering perilously low; that, in fact, this was his last chance; and that every month and week and day was important. It was not just a boyish impatience which spurred him on. It was a deep-rooted and perfectly sound instinct, warning him now as it warned him again and again during the Forty-five that he had not a moment to spare, and that any kind of retreat or postponement, however apparently justified, must be fatal to his cause. He knew he was engaged in a forlorn hope, and that it was not the business of a forlorn hope to pause or stand on the defensive.

As none of the leading men of the party agreed with him, he soon learned to keep his opinions to himself, though he never wavered in his intentions. "To go single," said the lukewarm Marischal, "unless you are invited by the principal peers [of England] both for credit and good sense would be for ever the destruction of the Cause." Needless to say, that was also James's view. In July 1744 Murray came over from Scotland and saw the Prince in Paris, where he was staying with Æneas Macdonald, the Jacobite banker. Charles told Murray plainly that he was determined to land in Scotland the following summer "if he brought only a single footman." And Murray, after warning him that he could not rely upon the support of more than four or five thousand Highlanders, hastened back to Scotland with this alarming news. Personally he seems to have agreed with the Prince and to have encouraged him in his "mad project."

But the Scottish Jacobites were seriously alarmed. Nearly every leading man among them was strongly opposed to a landing without the backing of French regular troops. Six thousand men at least were required, they thought, with arms and money to correspond. Two forcible letters were addressed to Charles, placing this view before him. By a strange series of accidents neither of them ever reached him. Instead of a reply, the Scottish Jacobites received a bundle of commissions for those who were to serve as officers in the Prince's army and an intimation that Charles himself expected to be with them in June. Murray was hurriedly despatched to the West Highlands to intercept the boy and persuade him to go back. But Murray could get no news of him, and so returned to Edinburgh. The situation had its comic side. It seemed impossible that a rebellion begun in this spirit could end in anything but fiasco.

Charles meanwhile went on quietly with his plans. He carefully concealed his intentions from his father. He would have ignored the warning letters from the Scottish lords even if he had received them. He was relying upon his "loyal Highlanders," whom he had not yet seen. And his instinct, as it turned out, was right.

He was running into debt, but he managed to purchase about a thousand muskets, eighteen hundred broad-swords, and a few small field-pieces. He had in money 4000 louis d'or, and a Mr Anthony Walsh, a rich Irish merchant, had fitted out a small vessel of fourteen guns, the *Doutelle*, which was to convey him to Scotland. Another Irish merchant, a Mr Walter Rutlidge, of Dun-kirk, had commissioned a more imposing vessel, the *Elizabeth* (sixty guns), commanded by Captain D'O, to act as escort.

On the 21st of June, 1745, at a little fishing village near the mouth of the Loire, Prince Charles embarked on the *Doutelle* for the reconquest of his kingdom. He had exactly seven companions in the adventure, and the names of these seven men were William Murray, Marquis of Tullibardine (and the Jacobite Duke of Atholl); Sir Thomas Sheridan, the Prince's former tutor; Sir John Macdonald, described as a captain in the Carabineers; Colonel John William O'Sullivan; Mr George Kelly; Mr Francis Strickland, another former tutor; and Mr Æneas Macdonald, the banker. There were also on board a man named Buchanan, who lived with Æneas Macdonald and had been employed as a Jacobite messenger between England and France, and Duncan Cameron of Barra.

Contrary winds detained them for a week at Bell-Ile. Here they were joined by the *Elizabeth*, and the two ships set sail together on the 4th of July, shaping a course round the west coast of Ireland for the Hebrides. The weather was mild now, and with a brisk favouring wind, apparently in the east-south-east, the two vessels, with all sails set, danced gaily over the sea to Skye, while the lad who was born to be King walked eagerly up and down the quarterdeck of the *Doutelle*, straining his eyes northward.

But Skye was a long way off, and England lay between

and though the Lords of the Admiralty, slumbering at
Whitehall, had taken no special precautions to prevent
such a "mad project" as this, the chances were always
against making a voyage through these waters without
receiving some attention from the British fleet. When
they were five or six days out a man-of-war, afterwards
identified as H.M.S. *Lion*, hove in sight, and "came
pretty near them," evidently regarding them with some
suspicion. She dropped astern, but next morning she
appeared again, and, according to the log of the *Doutelle*,
other English ships were sighted on the southern hori-
zon. It became obvious that the Frenchmen were being
pursued.

When the *Lion* had got to within a league and a half on
the starboard (or windward) quarter the French ships
cleared for action, and, "the chaplain having given
absolution," the *Doutelle*, with the Prince on board,
approached the *Elizabeth* within speaking distance. The
two captains held a hurried consultation, the upshot of
which was that as soon as the *Lion* and the *Elizabeth*
were engaged at close quarters, the little *Doutelle*
should close the *Elizabeth* and put fifty men on board
of her, and the *Elizabeth* should then attempt to
board the *Lion*, that being their best hope of victory
in view of the superior gunnery of the English.
Having done this, the *Doutelle* was to continue her
voyage to Scotland. Prince Charles and Anthony Walsh,
the Irish owner of the *Doutelle*, who was also on board,
subscribed to this plan. There are other less likely
versions of this incident. One (Duncan Cameron's)
makes the Prince insist upon the *Doutelle* joining in the
sea fight against the *Lion*, and says that Walsh, with the
approval of the Prince's companions, threatened to send
him down to his cabin unless he agreed to an immediate breakaway for Scotland. The captain's log of the

Doutelle seems rather unnecessarily to emphasize that it was "by the Prince's order" that they set a course for Scotland—it protests too much. On the other hand, it is quite unlike Charles to have allowed himself to be bullied in this way. The Whig version, which is to the effect that he sat trembling in his cabin and never came on deck till the firing was finished, may be disregarded.

But the captain of the *Lion* upset all calculations by his seamanlike handling of his ship. After exchanging a few broadsides with the *Elizabeth* he hoisted his jib and ran ahead, with the evident intention of getting across her bows. Captain D'O attempted to foil him by doing the same thing, but, says the *Doutelle's* log-book:

> The *Elizabeth* having delayed a little in executing the same manœuvre, the Englishman had time to pass forward and contrived so well that he fired all his port broadside, which raked the *Elizabeth* fore and aft, and must have killed many and done her great damage, so that the Englishman got between our two ships, and fired from his starboard guns three shots, which passed between my masts; my sails were riddled with his small shots, so much so that we did not fire, being out of range to reach him with our small guns.

The *Lion* and the *Elizabeth* again changed places, and, for some reason, steered south-east, still exchanging broadsides, while the little *Doutelle* followed nervously, expecting every moment to fall into the hands of the other English ships which had been seen to the southward. It was now getting dark, however, and at 10 P.M. the firing ceased, and the *Doutelle* was able to approach and speak her consort. She was told that the *Elizabeth* was badly damaged, Captain D'O was among the wounded, and his second-in-command announced his intention of immediately making for Brest. Whereupon "by the Prince's order" the *Doutelle* put about and continued her course alone to Scotland.

It was an heroic resolution, and when, a few hours later, they sighted two English ships of war it looked as though they might have to pay dearly for it. But a thin mist luckily intervened, and when it cleared a little there was nothing in sight. Every hour now they were drawing nearer to Scotland. Just before they sat down to dinner in the great cabin an eagle appeared and hovered over the ship. Tullibardine thought it was a good omen. "The king of birds," he said to Charles, "is come to welcome your Royal Highness on your arrival in Scotland."

But now, through the thin mist, they could distinguish the rugged coastline of the Long Isle. And these seven men (ever afterwards to be known as the Seven Men of Moidart, from the name of their landing-place on the mainland) crowded to the bulwarks, and there, with their Prince, all wrapped up to the eyes in their cloaks, gazed hungrily at the land. Says the ship's log:

> When they were near the shore of the Long Isle, Duncan Cameron was set out in the long boat to fetch them a proper pilot. When he landed he accidentally met with Barra's piper, who was his old acquaintance, and brought him on board. The piper piloted them safely into Erisca.

And at Eriskay Prince Charlie went over the side and was pulled ashore in the longboat, and stepped out on the rocky foreshore, swept by the cold salt spray. The Forty-five had begun.

CHAPTER IV

THE RAISING OF THE STANDARD

THERE was nothing in sight but a "mean, low hut" belonging to some fishermen, and they stumbled over the rocks towards it. The place where they landed has ever since been called Coilleag a' Phrionnsa, or the Prince's Strand, and "a pink convolvulus, not elsewhere known on the island, is said to have sprung from some seeds which happened to be in the pocket of his jacket."[1] There was nothing for them to eat in the hut; "they could not find a grain of meal or one inch of bread." "But," says Æneas Macdonald, who was of the party, "they catched some flounders which they roasted upon the bare coals."

Duncan Cameron stood cook. "The Prince sat at the cheek of the little ingle upon a fail sunk (or heap of peats), and laughed heartily at Duncan's cookery." Duncan admits that he did it "awkwardly enough." There was no chimney in the hut, except a hole in the middle of the roof, and, what with the smoke from the fire and the fumes from the roasting fish, the Prince was "almost choked," and kept dashing to the door for a breath of fresh air; until their fisherman landlord, who had no idea of his identity, called out to know "What the plague is the matter with that fellow, that he can neither sit nor stand still, and neither keep within nor without doors?"

However, the flounders were cooked and eaten at last, and as night had now fallen, and with it a heavy and

---

[1] Andrew Lang.

persistent downpour of rain, and as many of the party were tired, there was a general move towards bed. The Prince was the cheeriest of them all, and, seeing that there were very few beds available in this fisherman's hut, he insisted that those of his companions who were most fatigued should forthwith occupy them. Taking his tutor, Sir Thomas Sheridan, by the arm, he led him to the humble couch which had been allotted to himself, and after examining it somewhat narrowly he persuaded Sir Thomas to get in, at the same time announcing his own intention of sitting up all night. Whereat the landlord, Angus Macdonald, exclaimed indignantly that it was a bed fit for a prince—and wondered to hear them all laugh. So passed the first night in Scotland.

The next morning dawned clear and fine, and in that clean, invigorating air Prince Charles, who was young enough not to notice the loss of a night's sleep, immediately proceeded to get in touch with those he thought might prove to be his friends. He had landed on a tiny, insignificant island. To the south of him was Barra, Duncan Cameron's home; to the north the important island of South Uist, owning allegiance to Macdonald of Clanranald; beyond that North Uist, ruled by Macdonald of Sleat; and to the north of that again Lewis, inhabited by Mackenzies and Macleods; and to the north-west Skye, with more Macleods and Macdonalds of Sleat; while Rum and Eigg lay almost due east, between him and the mainland.

As a first move he sent for Alexander Macdonald of Boisdale, in South Uist, stepbrother of Clanranald. Macdonald, a cautious, middle-aged person, hastened down to his boat and soon came bobbing over the water to Eriskay. He was nervous and anxious, not quite understanding whom he was to meet, but probably fearing the worst. The interview must have been sufficiently

damping for the young Prince. Macdonald was loyal to
the core; but when Charles discovered himself and stated
the force he had brought with him he immediately began
to implore him to "go home again."

"I am come home, sir," replied the Prince.

He went on to say that, having landed in Scotland,
nothing on earth would induce him to turn back until
he had put his just cause to the arbitrament of arms—a
resolution which he kept. And, casting about in his
mind for the names of local chieftains likely to be friendly,
he mentioned to Boisdale that Sir Alexander Macdonald
of Sleat and the Laird of Macleod were reported to have
committed themselves in advance (this is very doubtful)
and that he proposed to send messengers to them. Boisdale told him that he had "pitched upon the wrong
persons," for neither of them in his opinion would raise
a hand for the Cause. But he agreed to the sending of
the messengers and suggested that the result of these
inquiries might be taken as a "test."

In the meantime Æneas Macdonald had persuaded the
Prince to take ship to the mainland and visit the
Laird of Kinlochmoidart, Æneas's brother; and they
arrived at Borradale, in Moidart, on the following day,
July 25. The news of the Prince's arrival was beginning
to get about, and as the ship lay at anchor small knots of
people began to assemble on the beach, and first one
Highland chief, then another, arrived and had himself
rowed out to the vessel.

Charles needed consolation, for his first two shots had
gone badly astray. Neither Macdonald of Sleat nor the
Laird of Macleod took the trouble to answer his letters.
The former had instantly written to warn the Govern-
ment of his arrival, referring to him as "the pretended
Prince of Wales" and to his followers as "madmen."
Macleod did nothing for the moment, but later wrote

to the Lord President, Duncan Forbes, that he and Macdonald of Sleat were using all their influence with their neighbours against "this mad rebellious attempt."

It is to be noted, however, that they always referred to the rebellion as "mad," never as wicked or disloyal. Indeed, their defence of their attitude, as they later explained to the Jacobite emissaries, was simply that the Prince had failed to carry out the stipulations laid down by his friends in Scotland, had brought no French soldiers nor munitions of war, and that to join him was to commit suicide. Even in their letters to President Forbes protesting their loyalty the theme is always dislike of the rebellion rather than love of King George.

The Prince stood on the deck of his little vessel in Loch-na-Nuagh, looking towards the shore, waiting for the answer of his loyal Highlanders. His slim figure was clothed in black from head to foot, and he looked rather like a priest—which, indeed, he gave himself out to be. It was only forty-eight hours since he first set foot in Scotland, but it was astonishing how he had got things moving.

Macdonald of Kinlochmoidart was crossing the waters of Lochy, when he chanced to meet Mr Hugh Macdonald, brother of the Laird of Morar and Roman Catholic Bishop of Diana (Numidia). "What news?" he asked. "No news at all have I," said Bishop Hugh. "Then," said Kinlochmoidart, "I'll give you news: you'll see the Prince this night at my home." "What prince do you mean?" asked Hugh. "Prince Charlie," said Kinlochmoidart. "You are certainly joking," protested the other. He went on to ask how many men the Prince had brought with him—to which Kinlochmoidart had to answer, "Seven"—what stock of arms and money and so forth, and said bluntly that he did not like the look of

PRINCE CHARLES AT THE TIME OF THE FORTY-FIVE
From a miniature in the collection of the Earl of Wemyss
By permission of the Hon. Sir Evan Charteris, K.C.   68

things. Kinlochmoidart answered: "I cannot help it; if the matter goes wrong, then I will certainly be hanged, for I am engaged already."[1]

Bishop Hugh was one of Prince Charles's first visitors next day. He appears to have urged him almost tearfully to return to France, but, finding that line of conversation unprofitable, he contented himself with warning the Prince to be exceedingly careful of his person, for "the Campbells in the neighbourhood would be too ready to take him and give him up to his enemies." "I have no fear about that at all," replied Charles briefly. The Bishop must have been completely won over by Charles's personal charm, for the next we hear of him he is blessing the blue and golden standard at Glenfinnan; and he dies a Jacobite exile in France. At this point, according to Lord Elcho, even those who had come with Charles on the boat from France were in favour of returning—all except Sir Thomas Sheridan.

Now, the point to notice in all these preliminary discussions is the steady, determined attitude of the young Prince. John Murray of Broughton, who was probably the shrewdest critic of events on the Jacobite side, has well observed that, "had the Chevalier seemed the least daunted by the apparent caution of his friends, or agreed to their not raising in arms for some time, and keep'd the ship hovering off the coast for a retreat," it is "more than probable" that Macdonald of Sleat, the Macleod, and Lord Lovat (another doubter) would have communicated their own selfish fears to many other people, so that in the end a landing would have become impossible, and there would be nothing left for Charles to do but sail back to France, with his skin whole but his character

---

[1] He was hanged at Carlisle in 1746. It is astonishing and edifying to note how many of the Prince's early supporters went in with him in this spirit—hardly hoping for victory, but willingly offering their lives in what seemed to them a just cause.

and his Cause lost for ever. But he stood out—at first almost alone—against the defeatists, and, just because he knew his own mind and was prepared to risk his all, he —young as he was, a mere boy in looks—easily dominated the situation. Even the slow James, the Old Pretender, in Rome, who was so little capable himself of any such gesture, so cautious that his son had never dared to tell him that a landing was contemplated—even James, when he heard what had happened, was stirred to exclaim that Charles's action, though rash, "would always do him honour."

But now the stout and loyal men began to arrive. Young Ranald Macdonald of Clanranald on the 26th of July, and soon after Clanranald himself, Alexander Macdonald of Glenalladale, Æneas Macdonald of Dalily, and many others, came to the village of Forsy and signalled from the beach for the ship's boat to fetch them aboard. One of them has left behind him an anonymous diary[1] from which we discover nothing of himself except that he served as an officer in the Jacobite army, but which gives a most convincing and moving account of the appearance of the young Prince at this outset of his gallant adventure.

He says that they found a large tent pitched upon the ship's deck, "well furnished with variety of wines and spirits and light refreshment." He and his party were greeted there by the Marquis of Tullibardine, with whom some of them had been out in the Fifteen. They stood in the tent talking and drinking, and suddenly Clanranald was a-missing, having, as they understood, been called down to the Prince's cabin. It was given out that no one else could expect to see Charles that night; but there was electricity in the air, for, as the diarist says, they were all "overjoyed to find themselves so near their long-

[1] *The Lockhart Papers* (1817).

wished-for Prince." (We have to remember those thirty weary years of waiting.)

At last Clanranald returned and stood talking with his friends and with the Irish adventurers and others who sat about under the awning. And then there entered the tent, unannounced, a tall youth "in a plain black coat, with a plain shirt, not very clean, and a cambrick stock fixed with a plain silver buckle, a fair round wig out of the buckle, a plain hat with a canvas string having one end fixed to one of his coat buttons; he had black stockings and brass buckles in his shoes." And, says the diarist, "at his first appearance I felt my heart swell to my very throat."

The strange youth bowed courteously to the assembled company, and was introduced by one of the Irishmen present as "ane English Clergyman who had long been possessed with the desire to see and converse with Highlanders." He came and sat on an oak chest near our diarist and made the latter sit down beside him, which he did, not without reluctance, for he suspected that he "might be one of more note than he was said to be." There followed a conversation of which it would be a pity to omit a line:

He asked me if I was not cold in that habite (viz., the Highland garb). I answered, I was so habituated to it that I should rather be so if I was to change my dress for any other. At this he laugh'd heartily, and next enquired how I lay with it at night, which I explained to him. He said that by wraping myself so closs in my plaid I would be unprepared for any sudden defence in the case of a surprise. I answered, that in such times of danger, or during a war, we had a different method of useing the plaid, that with one spring I could start to my feet with drawn sword and cock'd pistol in my hand without being in the least incumber'd with my bedcloaths. Several such questions he put to me; then rising quickly from his seat he calls for a dram, when the same person whisper'd me a second time to pledge the stranger but not to drink to him, by which seasonable hint I was confirm'd in my suspicion who he was. Having taken a glass of wine in his hand, he drank to us all round and soon after left us.

Now some of the best of Clanranald's men were enlisted as the Prince's personal bodyguard—the first troops raised in the Forty-five—while others were employed in unloading from the ship the arms and the money that Charles had brought with him. It was a busy scene on that obscure little beach miles from anywhere. It gave the tone to the whole affair: a rebellion in miniature, a provincial uprising, a concentration of the only natural fighting men in Great Britain, and a brief, fierce thrust by this tiny spearhead almost to the very heart of the great, apathetic country. They could make it wriggle, but they were not numerous enough to set a light to that spark of loyalty which still remained.

Donald Macdonald of Scotos came on board as Glengarry's representative, likewise Macdonald of Keppoch and Macdonald of Glencoe, whose people had been massacred under Dutch William's orders in 1692. And on the 4th of August arrived Donald Cameron of Lochiel, called by the Highlanders Young Lochiel (for his father was still alive, though attainted and in exile). He was the most important chief who had yet come to pay his respects to the Prince; he was always good for eight hundred men of his own clan, and his personal qualities had raised him to a high position in the Highlands and were to make him one of the most prominent figures in the Forty-five. Lochiel had been one of those who had written to Charles urging him not to come over without a body of foreign troops, but the letter, as we have seen, had gone astray. He was said to have been "a little troubled" when he received Charles's letter informing him of the landing. In fact, he shared the general opinion that the enterprise was almost hopeless. However, like the loyal man he was—and there is a surprising consensus of opinion, even among the squabbling chroniclers, as to the nobility of Lochiel's character —he hastened to obey the Prince's commands.

They met at Borradale—Lochiel, a grizzled veteran of fifty, the most loyal man in Scotland, but deeply perturbed in mind, anxious for the safety of his Prince, and Charles, young, eager, inspired, feeling success within his grasp, the one man of all that company who really knew his own mind. "Now or never is the word." And then there was his personal attraction. How could Lochiel resist? He would not have been a Highlander if he had. It is said that he urged the Prince to go back. Charles replied:

"In a few days, with the few friends that I have, I will erect the Royal Standard, and proclaim to the people of Britain that Charles Stuart is come over to claim the crown of his ancestors, to win it, or to perish in the attempt. Lochiel, who, my father has often told me, was our firmest friend, may stay at home, and learn from the newspapers the fate of his Prince."

"No," answered Lochiel, deeply moved, "I'll share the fate of my Prince, and so shall every man over whom nature or fortune has given me any power." This was one of the decisive moments of the Forty-five; for, as Home, the contemporary historian, tells us, it was universally agreed in Scotland that if Lochiel had refused to take up arms "the spark of rebellion must have instantly expired."

So the word went through the countryside, and the clans gathered slowly. It was rare for any one chief to assemble more than two hundred men. To Charles they must have seemed a heterogeneous collection. The Macdonalds of Moidart, among whom he had landed, were Roman Catholics; the Stuarts of Appin were Episcopalians; so were the Macdonalds of Glencoe, whose non-juring clergy were being persecuted by the Hanoverian Government.   Yet they were all united—first, by an instinctive feeling that this was the last fight of the clans to maintain their ancient customs and their right to carry arms; second, by a deep-seated community of race, as expressed in language and manners; third, and not least, by an affectionate and chivalrous loyalty towards the person of their gallant young Prince.

Charles had adopted Highland dress, and it became him to a marvel.   A bonnier lad never stepped among the heather, nor one more dangerously attractive—with that cunning mixture in his veins of Scottish and Continental blood.   In spite of the everlasting quarrels of their leaders, the cowardice and even treachery in high places, these two sentiments served to hold the clans together to the end—the feeling that their own existence was at stake and their personal devotion to Prince Charles. So the movement spread among the hills; and some one was busily stitching together a flag which Prince Charlie was to unfurl at Glenfinnan.

But what about Whig Scotland, the prosperous people of the plains, the quiet farmers, the bankers and businessmen, the dour descendants of the Covenanters who had waxed fat under the rule of good King George, burgesses of Edinburgh like Patrick Crichton, to whom Jacobites were so many "caterpillars," and all the solid, law-abiding citizens of the middle class, who loathed the sight of a Highlander as they would the devil?   These people would often come to their doorways during those summer months of 1745 and glance nervously towards the northern hills, now clothed in all the purple glory of the heather, and wonder what was happening behind them—whether there was any truth in these rumours that the clans were astir, whether that little sound now (did ye hear it?) was the skirl of the pipes.

And the small, inadequate garrison of English redcoats at Fort William, on Loch Linnhe, in the heart of the Cameron country, looked to their loopholes and their ammunition, and began to send messages southward to General Sir John Cope (commanding his Majesty's forces in Scotland) suggesting that something serious was afoot. One of these messages, dated August 2, stated definitely that Prince Charles had landed, and Cope immediately began to strengthen his garrisons, forming a camp at Stirling, where some 1700 foot and 600 dragoons were speedily collected. But his appeals to London for re-inforcements produced little result; most of King George's troops were engaged on the Continent, and the Government were slow to realize that this belated Jacobite effort was to prove more dangerous to them than the well-timed and apparently formidable rising of the Fifteen. So Cope was poorly supported and, like many British generals before and since his time, was left to bear the opprobrium of defeat, while the laurels of victory went to a more favoured successor with overwhelming forces at his command.

Here, obviously, was the opportunity of the French. A moderate force of regulars landed in Scotland might have changed the whole situation, might have formed a nucleus for the Jacobite clans, might have carried them southward and across the border in an irresistible wave before any adequate barrier had been thrown up. But the French did nothing! Perhaps it was partly the fault of the Jacobite ambassadors who, about this time, were sent to interview the French Minister, D'Argenson, on James's behalf. It would be hard to imagine a less impressive couple than the aged and doddering Lord Marischal, who had never believed in the rebellion, and the eccentric Lord Clancarty, the one-eyed Irish peer, who to the Frenchman was a mere figure of fun. He had lost his eye in a tavern brawl, when some one threw a bottle at his head. He was offensively dirty in his person. The elegant D'Argenson, while refusing all Clancarty's requests on behalf of Prince Charles, is said to have offered him instead the use of his private barber. As for Marischal, he had lived a long time in Spain and is jokingly described as a mixture of "Aberdeenshire and Valencia." They effected nothing.

But young Charles gave little thought to the talk of the diplomatists. There were things to be done. He was getting on famously with his Highlanders. He had even learned to propose King James's health in Gaelic. A rendezvous was appointed at Glenfinnan, at the head of Loch Shiel, on the nineteenth day of August; there Cameron of Lochiel, Macdonald of Keppoch, Clanranald, Stuart of Ardshiel, and "the principle gentlemen of Glengarry's family" were to have their people assembled, ready armed, and the Royal Standard was to be raised.

But first there was a little blood to be let. From Fort William, as we have seen, alarming messages had been despatched south and east reporting the gathering of the clans. Now the officer commanding the garrison at Fort Augustus, on Loch Ness, in Inverness-shire, conceived it his duty (he being farther to the eastward and therefore in less immediate danger) to send reinforcements to his colleague at Fort William before that post became entirely surrounded by hostile clans in arms. Accordingly two companies of the First Regiment of Foot (now the Royal Scots) set out from Fort Augustus on the 16th of August. It was a long and tiring march in the hot weather, and as the little column approached High Bridge, about eight miles from Fort William and the only means of crossing the rushing torrent of the

River Spean, there seems to have been no suspicion in anyone's mind that the Highlanders might have got between them and their destination. Captain John Scott, who commanded the two companies, was about to lead the way across the river when he heard the sound of bagpipes and "saw some Highlanders on the other side of the bridge skipping and leaping about with swords and firelocks in their hands." Scott halted his men and sent a sergeant and his own servant to find out who these people were; but as the messengers crossed the bridge two "nimble Highlanders" sprang out and seized them and carried them off as prisoners. If Scott had immediately pressed on he might have broken through to Fort William; but, not liking the look of things, nor knowing the strength of his opponents, he ordered his men to turn about and march back to Fort Augustus.

The Highlanders assembled at the bridge amounted, as a matter of fact, to not more than a dozen men led by Macdonald of Tiendrish. But Macdonald, as soon as he saw the soldiers, had sent off messages to the surrounding chiefs, and now, as Scott's two companies in their retreat entered the narrow road on the mountainside above Loch Lochy, the Highlanders gathered about them and began shooting down at them as they passed. The sound of the firing attracted more clansmen to the spot. Having got clear of the road, Scott perceived a strong body of Highlanders waiting for him at the end of the next loch (Loch Oich), and he therefore turned aside and crossed the isthmus between the two lakes, intending to throw himself into Invergarry, a place of some strength. But a party of Macdonalds of Glengarry appeared suddenly over the hillside and intercepted him, and the Macdonalds of Keppoch presently joined them. Seeing himself surrounded on all sides, Scott formed his men into a hollow square and attempted to continue his march. But the Highlanders increased in numbers at every moment, and at last Macdonald of Keppoch, advancing alone, called out to the soldiers to lay down their arms and their lives would be spared. The situation being quite hopeless, Scott surrendered, but not before two of his men had been killed and himself wounded. Lochiel arrived with his Camerons and took charge of the prisoners, whom he treated with great courtesy. The Highlanders had not lost a man, and were greatly elated at the result of this first engagement of the Forty-five.

Meanwhile Charles at Moidart had been having a difficult time. He was discovering some of the weaker points in the Highland character. The small supply of arms and money from his own ship had been somehow got ashore, but it had taken a long time. His new followers were more than willing to march up and down the beach all day, playing their bagpipes, cheering him whenever he appeared on deck, and drinking his health half the night in usquebaugh (whisky), but when it came to an ordinary job of work their attitude changed. Unloading a ship was no occupation, he must understand, for a Highland "shentleman." Our old acquaintance Mr Walsh, of the *Doutelle*, after leaving Charles on Eriskay, had intercepted two ships laden with oatmeal off the island of Skye, and had sent them into Moidart to assist the Prince in provisioning his army; but we have it on the best authority that only an infinitesimal portion of this useful cargo was ever got farther than the beach. In the meantime Charles was much occupied in writing round to all his friends, real and supposed, urging them to be present on the great occasion of the raising of the standard at Glenfinnan, fixed for the 19th of August.

He himself arrived there on the evening of the appointed day, escorted by three companies of Clanranald's men. John Murray of Broughton had joined him now, and he has left us a description of the scene. Glenfinnan is a narrow valley lying between high, craggy mountains. At each end the glen is shut in by lakes. The sun was already sinking when Charles arrived, and the valley seemed dim and almost empty. He stood with his small party of followers, Macdonalds and Stuarts, and looked eagerly at the surrounding mountains for the appearance of Lochiel and his men. If the Camerons defaulted his cause was lost indeed. There was a moment of acute anxiety. Then some one heard the sound of the pipes. The Camerons were seen approaching over the hills, first three men on the skyline, then three more. For they marched in two columns, three abreast, and between the columns walked the English redcoats, taken prisoner on the 16th, without their arms. Incidentally, half the Camerons also were without arms; but the sight of the gallant clan, nearly eight hundred strong, was exactly the stimulant that Charles had needed. He knew now that Lochiel was definitely on his side. The clansmen stood round him in their ranks in the failing light, while Tullibardine unfurled the Royal Standard, and James's commission appointing his son as his Regent was read aloud, in that distant valley, with all proper ceremony.

They had hardly finished with this ceremonial before Macdonald of Keppoch arrived with a further three hundred men, and a party of Macleods also, who came to say that they disowned the action of their chief and disclaimed him and would lay down their lives for the Cause. There were other flags displayed that day— among them surely that golden St Andrew's cross on a blue ground which was the clan colour of the Stuarts, and was later carried into battle at Culloden by Stuart of Ardshiel.[1]

[1] And might be seen by anybody who visited the Exhibition of Scottish Art and Antiquities in London in 1931.

And as Prince Charles saw his friends gathering around him at last he stood before them at the foot of the Royal Standard and made what one of his hearers has described as "a short but very pathetick speech." He said he would not descant upon his father's incontrovertible title to the throne, for he presumed that no one would be there present who did not agree as to that (he had forgotten the red-coated prisoners who stood listening), but would merely say that he was there not only to assert his rights, but to secure the welfare and happiness of his people and that he had deliberately landed in that part of the island of Great Britain where he knew he would be likely to find a number of brave gentlemen willing to help him in "so glorious an enterprise." With their assistance and that of a just God "Who never fails to avenge the cause of the injured" he "did not doubt of bringing the affair to a happy issue."

As he spoke he stared out over their heads to the southern hills, his young face tense and drawn, meaning every word he said in every fibre of his being. In his imagination he was already in London; already the Second Restoration was an accomplished fact; already he rode through the Strand, as his grand-uncle had before him on that May day in 1660, while all that was soundest and sweetest in the old loyal heart of England made him welcome.

He saw all that. And these wild Highlanders, looking at him, threw up their bonnets in the air, and cheered him so that the sound of it echoed all along the valley.

CHAPTER V

AT THE GATES OF EDINBURGH

GENERAL SIR JOHN COPE, Commander-in-Chief of his Majesty's forces in Scotland, has been unkindly described by a contemporary as "one of these ordinary men who are fitter for anything than the chief command in war, especially when opposed, as he was, to a new and uncommon enemy." Even the activity which he now displayed has been attributed by the same authority (Home) to a nervous desire to exhibit his zeal to the Ministers in London upon whose generosity he relied for his pension.

So far as can be seen at this distance of time that judgment is a little unfair. We get a picture of a sturdy, red-coated figure hurrying from post to post along the north-western border of the threatened Whig counties, exhorting his troops to do their duty, cursing them fluently in an English accent which men of London or Sussex could understand, making them feel that they were isolated there in a foreign country as strange and remote as America, supporting the cause of true-blue Protestantism and King George, and that they would certainly get their throats cut, or worse, unless they showed a brave front against the local savages.

At the first distant whisper of the pipes behind the northern hills Cope had come out boldly for that kind of defence which consists in taking the offensive from the start. Who can doubt now that he was right? Before the lucky accident of the skirmish at High Bridge, which inspired the Highlanders with a contempt for their opponents which they never quite lost, and even up to

the unfurling of the standard at Glenfinnan, which gave
the rebellion its first real inspiration and driving-force,
they were never at a strength which would have given
them a chance of withstanding the attack of a strong
body of regular troops. They were so ill-equipped that
they never attempted to attack the outlying garrisons of
Fort William and Fort Augustus; they marched warily
and in a wide circle round Inverness, like a dog round a
cat with its claws out. Cope's idea was to attack them
and break them before they outnumbered him hopelessly,
and the plan had at least enough sense in it to exclude
the suggestion of mere window-dressing. That it failed
was due less to any slackness on Cope's part than to the
backwardness of London in supporting him.

Cope, as we have seen, had formed a camp at Stirling.
He arrived there on the 19th of August, and on the very
next day began his march to the north. The forces
under his command consisted of three and a half battalions
of infantry and two regiments of cavalry. Most of the
infantry were young soldiers, raised in the year 1741; but
there was one battalion of veterans (the 6th, or Guise's),
which was dispersed among the forts and barracks in the
North. The two regiments of dragoons were Gardiner's
and Hamilton's, raised in 1715, and therefore regarded
as veterans; but Cope thought that cavalry would be a
mere encumbrance among the hills, and so left them
behind—Gardiner's at Stirling and Hamilton's at Leith,
to defend Edinburgh. There were other troops in Scotland, amounting to about nine companies, including the
regiment of Whig Highlanders raised by Lord Loudoun
but as yet unarmed, and the two companies of Royal
Scots who, as has been said, had been captured by the
Highlanders at the skirmish near Loch Oich. None of
these was available. Cope, therefore, started from Stirling
with not more than 1400 infantry, four field-pieces, and

a long train of wagons carrying provisions and arms for the northern garrisons.

But Cope was too late. If he seriously hoped to overwhelm the Jacobites before they were at full strength he was soon disillusioned. At Dalnacardoch, by Loch Ericht, he met a certain Captain Swetenham, of Guise's regiment, who had been captured by the rebels on the 14th, while on his way to Fort William to take command of the garrison. Swetenham had been led by his captors to Glenfinnan, and had stood there among the other English prisoners listening to the Pretender's proclamation. Two days later he was set free on parole, after being very civilly treated, and had hastened southward to meet Cope. He met him at Dalnacardoch on the 25th, and earnestly warned him of the rapidly growing strength of Prince Charles's army. After the raising of the standard the Prince had spent the night in "a little barn at the head of the loch." Next day he had marched to Kinlochiel, and thence to Fassefern and Moy (where John Murray of Broughton, who had joined him at Kinlochmoidart, was formally appointed his secretary). Among new recruits was Gordon of Glenbucket. Though the Prince was still weak in numbers, his position was growing stronger every day. It was his intention to meet Cope in the Corryarrack Pass. And Cope, now that he was at last within striking distance, did not much like the idea.

Both commanders, as a matter of fact, were faced by difficult decisions. The strategical situation was extraordinarily interesting. It is impossible to understand it without the aid of a map. The Prince was slightly the stronger of the two and had a definite moral advantage. Marching from Moy to Invergarry Castle on the 25th, he found a letter there from Lord Lovat, that wily old chief of the Frasers, assuring him of his personal though still concealed loyalty, and urgently advising him to advance against Inverness. Inverness was the chief military stronghold of the north-eastern Highlands. On the other hand, Tullibardine was in favour of a southern march towards Edinburgh, the capital, rousing the Atholl country on the way.

To seize the capital was a brilliant strategic conception. Inverness might very well be left to stew in its own juice. But Charles's forces were terribly scanty for such a purpose. And King George had just put £30,000 on his head.[1] While he was hesitating 260 Stuarts of Appin under Ardshiel marched into his camp, and on the next day at Aberchalder 400 Glengarry Macdonalds and 120 Macdonalds of Glencoe, with some of the Grants of Glenmoriston, joined up. The arrival of the Stuarts was probably decisive; at any rate, the plan of the dramatic southern march was forthwith adopted. An advance party was sent ahead to seize the Corryarrack Pass, and Cope, wisely declining battle, turned aside through Ruthven and made haste to get into Inverness.

The Highlanders swarmed through the pass. An attempt to seize the barracks at Ruthven (against the Prince's advice, says Murray of Broughton) was repulsed with loss, but they marched on unopposed to Dalwhinny and Dalnacardoch. Here Lochiel sent home 150 of his Camerons, since they were practically unarmed. On August 31st Charles's forces reached Blair Castle, in Atholl, and were there joined by Colonel John Roy Stuart; and on the same day Inversnaid Barracks were surprised by the Macgregors and eighty-nine soldiers taken. Also on that day George II arrived in London from Hanover.

The Prince entered Perth on the 4th of September,

[1] He, who always despised such methods, wanted to reply with a contemptuous £30 for the head of King George, but his advisers made him put it up to the same figure as the Hanoverian offer.

and at once had himself proclaimed Regent for his father, James VIII of Scotland and III of England. This was a decisive moment of the campaign. If the Highlanders had failed to support him now, his march southward must have been a mere foray. His followers had suffered considerable hardships. From the departure from Glen-finnan on the 20th of August to the arrival at Blair on the 31st they had subsisted entirely on scraps of beef roasted over wood fires among the heather. But not only were his numbers considerably swelled while he rested in Perth—so that he was able to detach Keppoch and Clanranald to rouse Dundee and proclaim his father there and bring back money and supplies to Perth—but it was at this point that he was joined by the two men who held the chief military commands in the rebellion—the Duke of Perth and Lord George Murray. Of the former the most that can be said is that he was an honest man and a moderately competent commander. The second may fairly be described as a strategical genius. In tactics he had nothing to do except loose his High-landers for their charge, and he sometimes chose positions singularly unsuited for such a purpose. But the ease with which he dodged and outmanœuvred the English generals on every occasion, marching up and down the country from Edinburgh to Derby with an absurdly inferior force, giving battle only when he chose, un-doubtedly marks him out as a strategist who might have done great things on a larger stage. Unfortunately he had occupied an official position at the outbreak of the rebellion and had hesitated before choosing his side. He never got on with Murray of Broughton, nor with the Irishmen who surrounded the Prince, and was always regarded by the latter with suspicion. He and the Duke of Perth were appointed generals, and O'Sullivan, one of the Seven Men of Moidart, was made Q.M.G.

At Perth also the Prince was joined by Robertson of Struan, with two hundred men, and paid a visit to Glenalmond to inspect the troops raised by the Duke of Perth. Here Macpherson of Cluny, who had been seized near Corryarrack and fetched along with them (probably a willing prisoner), was released and sent home. And here, too, the Prince heard the important news that Cope had left Inverness on the 4th of September for Aberdeen, and had ordered transports to meet him there at the port, obviously with the intention of taking ship to the Firth of Forth and occupying Edinburgh before the Highland army could seize it.

There were two courses open to the Prince—to make a dash northward and try to intercept Cope on his way to Aberdeen or to continue the race for Edinburgh with a good prospect of winning. He chose the latter—and, as it turned out, he was right, for Cope reached Aberdeen on the 11th and sailed on the 15th, so that he could hardly have been caught in any case. Thus it was decided. The clansmen turned their faces southward and, with pipes playing and flags flying, marched upon Edinburgh, leaving the North to take care of itself.

Prince Charlie rode a horse taken from Captain Swetenham. But when his army reached the Forth he jumped down and was the first to put foot in the water, leading his detachment across the ford. Gardiner's dragoons, who might have obstructed the landing, fell back before the clansmen—and continued to do so at every point in the march until, as we shall see, retreat became a fatal habit with them. At Stirling the citizens regaled Charles's men with wine. The English garrison attempted to entertain them with grape-shot, but they circled round the castle at a safe distance and went on towards Edinburgh. In every house in which the Prince lodged they will show you the room he slept in.

Approaching Linlithgow, Lord George Murray, Lochiel, Keppoch, Glengarry, and Ardshiel (led by the Prince himself, according to Murray of Broughton) made a forced march by night in the hope of surprising the elusive dragoons, but found them already gone.

In Edinburgh, as the Highlanders drew nearer, there was much perturbation and declamation and a fierce buzzing round the Whig beehives. The volunteers were turned out to the number of eight hundred men, but they had only "old crassey officers," and they walked like men going to their execution. Two-thirds of the male inhabitants of Edinburgh are said to have been Whigs; but it is agreed that nearly all the women were Jacobites, and there is nothing more damping to the ardour of the amateur soldier than the feeling that the girls are on the other side. There were no fluttering white handkerchiefs at the windows as the volunteers marched to their quarters at the orders of a Lord Provost who was himself so supine in the matter as to be suspected of Jacobite leanings. The first glimmering of real excitement was when the King's dragoons were seen galloping southward, in ignominious flight, along the ridge beyond the North Loch (which then ran up to the castle walls), where now are the modern Princes Street and George Street. They had exchanged a few pistol-shots with Charles's handful of horsemen at Colt Bridge, and this was the result. Derisive feminine laughter sped them on their way.

The Prince and his Highlanders were at Corstorphine, only two or three miles out to the south-west. The news went through the city like a flame from the Grassmarket to Canongate. The imminence of his approach had been carefully concealed from the mob. Public opinion, fickle, sentimental, unthinking, now swung over violently to his side. The only Whig leader with the strength

of character and conviction to stem that landslide—
Duncan Forbes, the Lord President—was at Inverness,
organizing the Hanoverian resistance in the North.
The rest retired bitterly into their shells. The volunteers
gave up their arms, hurried home, and assumed innocent
attitudes at the tea-table. General Guest, who was
in command of the King's troops in the castle, and had
recently celebrated his eighty-fifth birthday, closed the
gates and prepared for a determined resistance. His
second-in-command, General Preston, who was eighty-
six, supported him heartily. Fortunately, the Prince
had no artillery.

The Prince was at the gates. He had sent a peremptory
summons to the Provost and magistrates, demanding the
admission of his army and the handing over of all military
stores, and had given them only two or three hours
to decide. But when the Provost and magistrates were
assembled in the Council Chamber and were on the very
point of agreeing to the Prince's demand, news was
brought to them that Cope's transports from Aberdeen
had just been sighted off Dunbar, and that as soon as the
wind abated a little he intended to make a landing there
and march to the relief of Edinburgh. Cope had lost
the race by a short head, but he might still intervene
within the next forty-eight hours; and these Edinburgh
wobblers, hardly one of whom was not prepared to cut
his coat to suit the cloth, determined to try a little
diplomacy. After deliberating most of the night they
sent out a deputation at two o'clock in the morning of
the 17th of September, and these men, stumbling about
the Prince's camp in the darkness, found Lord George
Murray and induced him to go in to the Prince and second
their request for a further delay. Charles peremptorily
refused, and sent word to the deputation to get them
gone. Lord George Murray's unfortunate attitude in

this matter must have deepened the Prince's distrust of him. According to Murray of Broughton, Charles understood perfectly well that the deputies were attempting to gain time pending Cope's arrival. Indeed, no sooner had they left the camp than he sent after them Murray of Broughton and Lochiel's Camerons with instructions to rush in if possible at the first peep of dawn and seize the town.

But though, as we have said, the Prince was at the gate, there remained the question of which gate. The famous West Port, the nearest at hand, nestled under the shade of the castle rock, and any Jacobite army attempting to enter there would be shot to pieces by General Guest's guns. From that point the ancient city wall took a long twist south, and then again north to the Bristo (Greyfriars) Port, which was still unpleasantly near the castle; and from thence eastward to Potterrow Port, at Kirk-o'-fields, and onward in the same direction to the Pleasants, whence it sloped north-eastward to Blackfriars and the Netherbow, separating the High Street from Canongate.

It was still just dark when Lochiel and Murray, with their men, came in sight of the walls, and they very wisely edged away from the castle towards their right, until they turned the corner and, passing through the Pleasants, came outside the gate called the Netherbow. Day was breaking, but they concealed themselves as well as they could while Murray and Lochiel held a hurried conversation. One of their number, disguised in a great coat and hunting cape, went to the gate, but was refused admission by the guard. It was decided to retreat, and Murray had actually gone to the rear of the column to guide them to the shelter of a hill near by, when, to Lochiel's delight, the Netherbow was suddenly thrown wide open to permit the egress of an important-looking coach. It was the magistrates' deputation again. They had been instructed to try the Prince once more with some further shilly-shallying, and had chosen for their point of departure the very gate at which Lochiel and his men were still waiting.

As the coach came out Lochiel and some of his leading Highlanders rushed in. In a moment the gate was seized and the guard disarmed. The Camerons, not knowing what resistance they might expect (in fact there was none), advanced at the double, with drawn swords and targets raised, setting up "a hideous yell," which was "their particular manner of making ane attack." And when the citizens of Auld Reekie, roused from their beds by the din, ran to their upper windows and looked down, they saw below them the blue bonnets and the white cockades streaming through the narrow streets and wynds. Edinburgh had fallen.

We have said that there was no resistance, yet old Edinburgh was one of the easiest places in the world in which to organize a street fight, and it had seen more than one of them in its time. In those steep, twisting lanes, with here and there a barricaded close, the Highlanders, accustomed to the open hills and many of them without firearms, might have spent an uncomfortable morning—or longer—if the Whigs had shown fight. The tall houses were let off in flats, and you could never be sure whether the heads looking down on you belonged to friends or foes. There was a surprising democracy in this higgledy-piggledy life. A countess would inhabit one floor of a house, a lodging-house keeper would live below her, and a retired fishmonger just above. It was almost modern in spirit—except that in these days it was the peeress who counted politically, whereas now it would probably be the fishmonger. The Canongate was the fashionable quarter, and Holyrood stood without

THE NETHERBOW PORT, EDINBURGH

This gate stood until 1794 at the lower end of the High Street, dividing it from
the Canongate, which was outside the city bounds.

90

the walls. There was little accommodation for Charles's army, for, though drinking shops were numerous, inns were "few and notoriously bad and dirty."[1]

In this conquered city the "wild Highlanders," whose well-known addiction to rape, arson, and even cannibalism had been freely noised about by the local Whig Press, behaved in a manner which is now generally admitted to have been exemplary. They were "civil and inno-cent"—no doubt acting under orders—"beyond what even their best friends could have expected." The Whig historians admit all this, but do not seem to like the Highlanders any the better for it. Says Patrick Crichton of Woodhouselee, a pious, combative Presby-terian:

> I entered the town by the Bristol Port which I saw to my indignation in the keeping of these caterpillars. A boy stood with a rusty drawen sword, and two fellows with things licke guns of the 16th Century sat on each syde the entry to the poors howse, and these were catching the vermin from their lurking places about their plaids and throwing them away. I said to Mr Jardine, Minister of Liberton, "Are these the scown-deralls have surprised Edinburgh by treachery?" He answered, "I had reither seen it in the hands of Frenchmen, but the divell and the deep sea are both bad."

Passing on through Cowgate and the High Street, Crichton found a great press of people before him, for James VIII and his son, the Prince Regent, were about to be proclaimed at the Cross, and all Edinburgh, Whig or Jacobite, seemed determined to be present. Crichton succeeded in getting into a house on the north side of High Street, from the windows of which he could look down on the animated scene in Parliament Close. There he saw "these mountain officers," with "their bag-pipes and loosie crew," march down from the Close to the

[1] Blaikie, *Edinburgh at the Time of the Occupation of Prince Charles* (1909).

Cross, the pipes playing merrily, and form a wide circle for the reading of the proclamation. He sneers at their equipment, their firearms of all shapes and sizes, some of "innormowows length," some tied together with string, their pitchforks and scythes, and the old Lochaber axes; but concludes that this was probably arranged on purpose to give a democratic appearance to the parade. Democratic it certainly was. After the herald, in a strong voice (Crichton could hear him plainly in the High Street), had read out James's proclamation promising political amnesty, removal of unpopular taxes, and the security of the established religion, printed copies of the announcement were passed round among the crowd; the wife of Murray of Broughton distributed white favours; and the Highlanders marched away to their quarters to the accompaniment of such cheers as left little doubt as to the sympathies of the mob.

In the meantime the Prince was approaching with the main body, and came in sight from the city walls about ten o'clock. In order to avoid the guns of the castle he took an even wider sweep to the right than Lochiel had done, and, passing right round the walls, he came in by Duddingston and under Arthur's Seat to the park behind Holyrood, where he found a vast number of people assembled and others streaming out through the city gates to welcome him. Curiosity to see the Prince had indeed risen to fever-heat—without distinction of sex or class or even politics. He did not disappoint them. His large brown eyes, fresh complexion freckled from the sun, and pointed chin, his natural charm and dignity—all these appear again in the records of friend and foe alike. "He was in the prime of youth," says a Whig historian, "tall and handsome, of a fair complexion" —one or two of his enemies have tried to give him red hair[1]—"he had a light-coloured periwig with his own hair combed over the front; he wore the Highland dress, that is, a tartan short coat without the plaid, a blue bonnet on his head, and on his breast the Star of the Order of St Andrew." According to one authority, he wore crimson velvet breeches and military boots; but another speaks of tartan "trews." All are agreed about the short tartan coat, the blue bonnet, and the Star of St Andrew.

So he stood in the park for a little that the people might see their bonnie prince; and then, mounting his horse, rode gracefully down the Duke's Walk to the gates of Holyrood while the crowd pressed forward, seeking to kiss his hand. There he dismounted again, and walked forward alone before the spectators towards the steps that led up to the wide open door of the palace of his ancestors. Perhaps he hesitated. There was little in him of theatricality, but he may well have paused a moment now. This was the opportunity for James Hepburn of Keith, who had been out in the Fifteen, to make himself a niche in history. Springing forward from among the onlookers, he snatched his sword from its scabbard, and, holding it high above his head, he preceded the Prince up the steps, and so into the Palace. The doors closed behind them.

---

[1] They say also that he had a "long visage" and "melancholy," "much sunburnt and freckled," with other such disparaging remarks, but always end up with the admission that he was an exceptionally "good-looking man," with "a figure and presence . . . not ill suited to his lofty pretensions."

CHAPTER VI

HEY, JOHNNIE COPE!

ALL that day, and all night too, the crowd stood densely packed in the outer court of the Palace of Holyrood, only moving aside now and then to leave a clear passage for the coaches and sedan chairs of the great gentlemen and ladies (especially the ladies) of Edinburgh who came to call upon the young Prince. Every time Charles appeared at the window there was a loud huzza. "Yet," remarks Lord Elcho bitterly, "not one of the mob who were so fond of seeing him ever ask'd to enlist in his service, and when he marched to fight Cope he had not one of them in his army." This is a common enough characteristic among city mobs, and Elcho, when he wrote those words, was an embittered man, hating the very memory of Prince Charlie and the Forty-five. But it is unfortunately true that he himself was one of the very few recruits obtained in Edinburgh.

Next morning, however, Lord Nairn arrived with a thousand Atholl men and encamped outside at Duddingston, covering the eastern approaches, and bringing the total strength of the Highland army up to somewhere about three thousand men. Also on this same morning the Prince sent Elcho to interview the Edinburgh magistrates and obtain from them, by force if necessary, a supply of new shoes, tents, and other equipment for his followers. Yet the whole affair was still on an almost absurdly miniature scale. A visit to the small house in White Horse Close, still standing to-day, which comfortably contained Prince Charlie's G.H.Q. brings the picture to life, and at the same time sets it in its true proportions—a handful of officers with two or three thousand wild Highlanders, almost lost to sight in a city of fifty or sixty thousand inhabitants, dominated by the grey walls of the castle, which was still held for King George.

Now, on the very same day that saw Prince Charles's triumphant entry in Edinburgh, and actually while his father's proclamation was being read at the Market Cross, Sir John Cope was disembarking his troops on the beach at Dunbar. He found there the two regiments of dragoons before mentioned who had come in that morning, rather flustered and dishevelled from their series of rapid movements to the rear, and altogether, as a Whig historian puts it, "in a condition not very respectable." As Cope watched the slow unloading of his transports he must have reflected gloomily that his numerical superiority in cavalry (the Prince had only about fifty horsemen all told) would probably make little difference when it came to a fight. It was about this time that a few (a very few) Whig volunteers from Edinburgh began to dribble in to Dunbar. Among them was Alexander Carlyle, later a Presbyterian minister and one of the chroniclers of the Rebellion, who immediately sought out Colonel Gardiner, commanding Gardiner's dragoons. He has left it on record that Gardiner told him: "Sandie, I have not above ten men in my regiment whom I am certain will follow me; but we must give them battle now, and God's will be done!"

So Johnnie Cope came rushing on his fate. There is a well-known Jacobite song:

> Cope sent a challenge frae Dunbar:
> "Charlie, meet me an ye daur,
> And I'll learn you the art o' war
>   If you'll meet me i' the morning."

Hey, Johnnie Cope, are ye waukin' yet?
Or are your drums a-beating yet?
If ye were waukin' I wad wait
*   To gang to the coals i' the morning.*

When Charlie looked the letter upon
He drew his sword the scabbard from:
" Come, follow me, my merry, merry men,
    And we'll meet Johnnie Cope i' the morning."
        Hey, Johnnie Cope . . .

" Now, Johnnie, be as good's your word;
Come, let us try baith fire and sword;
And dinna flee like frichted bird
    That's chased frae its nest in the morning."
        Hey, Johnnie Cope . . .

When Johnnie Cope he heard o' this
He thocht it wadna be amiss
To hae a horse in readiness
    To flee awa' in the morning.
        Hey, Johnnie Cope . . .

.   .   .   .

When Johnnie Cope to Berwick cam',
They speired at him, "Where's a' your men?"
" The deil confoond me gin I ken,
    For I left them a' i' the morning."
        Hey, Johnnie Cope . . .

.   .   .   .

The suggestion of personal cowardice contained in this lively ditty seems to have no foundation in fact. Cope was a brave, resolute officer, not even conspicuously incompetent—a little lacking in imagination and adaptability perhaps, but that much could be said of a good many comparatively successful generals. Certainly there was no idea of impending defeat in his head. Whatever he may have thought about the appearance of the dragoons, there was no reason why he should distrust the ability of his infantry to deal with this rabble of half-armed Highlanders. Home, the Whig historian, had just arrived at Dunbar, and assured him that there were not above two thousand Highlanders in Edinburgh (he had left before the arrival of the Atholl men). It was unfortunate, of course, that he was without regular artillerymen, so that his guns had to be manned by four old soldiers and a few sailors from the fleet. Still, the possession of these six field-pieces gave him another material advantage over his ill-armed opponent. In numbers the opposing sides were about equal.

Since it was now clear that the race for Edinburgh had been lost, the disembarkation proceeded at a leisurely pace, and it was not till the 19th of September that Cope was ready to move. Between Dunbar and Edinburgh, but much nearer to Dunbar, the land swells out into a broad peninsula, now the holy land of the game of golf. To march round the coast would be an obvious waste of time (though it would have left him with only one unprotected flank, since his right would rest upon the seashore), so Cope cut across the base of the peninsula and, on the night of the 19th, encamped in a field to the west of Haddington. Next morning he followed the same route and soon came out upon the coast road leading direct to Edinburgh, along the picturesque banks of the Firth of Forth.

" This little army," we are told, " made a great show —the cavalry, the infantry, the cannon, with a long train of baggage carts extended for several miles along the road." The flags were flying and the drums beating; from all accounts it was a bright early autumn day; and Cope, as he rode up and down the column, can hardly have doubted that these disciplined, well-equipped troops of his would make short work of the clansmen if they met them in the open. Nearer to Edinburgh, it is true, the hills rose abruptly, almost from the water's side: it might

G

be awkward to meet them there. But here, as his men marched through Port Seton and Cockenzie, was a wide prospect of open country, more or less flat, in which regular troops might deploy at their leisure. And at that moment came Lord Loudoun, who had been sent ahead to reconnoitre, galloping in with the news that the rebels were in full march from Edinburgh, and might be expected at any moment. Cope thought that the plain which he saw before him, between Seton and Preston, was "a very proper piece of ground to receive them," and he therefore marched on a little, halted, and drew up his men—the infantry in the centre, the dragoons on either flank, and the guns at the extreme left, or inland end, of the line. Nothing could have happened more fortunately. Instead of being attacked in the defiles, instead of having to force his way through the narrow streets of Edinburgh, here he was waiting for the enemy on his own chosen ground.

On the same day that Cope left Dunbar the Prince at Holyrood heard of it. He immediately withdrew the guards from the city gates, amounting to some hundreds of men, and himself went to Duddingston, and spent the night there—in a house they will show you now. By nine o'clock the next morning the whole army was drawn up at Duddingston, ready to march. Volunteers from Edinburgh were few, but among them was a group of surgeons with the necessary medical stores. Prince Charles, whose humanity and care for the wounded was one of his most attractive characteristics, had given personal attention to this detail of equipment usually ignored by Highland armies. Thanks to him, there was a good supply of coaches and light chaises for the conveyance of what we should call stretcher cases. Everything being ready, he went to the head of the line, and, according to Lord George Murray, who commanded under him, he made his followers a brief speech, with "a very determined countenance." "Gentlemen," he said, "I have flung away the scabbard; with God's assistance, I don't doubt of making you a free and happy people. Mr Cope shall not escape us as he did in the Highlands."

Lord George Murray led the van. He was anxious to prevent Cope from getting on to the high ground farther inland, and therefore kept well away from the coast road and pressed forward eagerly across the fields, looking always to the left for a first sight of the enemy. As he marched into Tranent he saw them below him on the coastal plain, and knew that his first objective had been gained. Murray had Lochiel's Camerons with him at the head of the column; and now, as he tells us, the Prince's Irish friend, O'Sullivan, came up and took fifty of these men and posted them in the churchyard at the foot of the village of Tranent, quite close to the enemy. Cope, as we have seen, had his guns at this inland end of his line; he now turned them upon the churchyard, and the Camerons were beginning to lose heavily when Murray sent and withdrew them. The incident vexed him, as his own journal shows. It was one of the first of an interminable series of quarrels between this able commander and the Prince's *entourage*.

Murray, then, was at Tranent. Below him stretched a belt of marshy land, difficult to cross; beyond that the coastal plain. To the left, in the plain, lay the villages of Preston and—nearer the sea—Prestonpans; on the right Cockenzie and Seton. Between the two the royal army was drawn up in its ranks, still facing towards Edinburgh. But as Cope became aware that the Highlanders were on the high ground threatening his left flank he swung round facing south, with the sea at his back. It was now getting dark, and he advanced his cavalry pickets to the edge of

99

the marsh, and ordered fires to be lit in front of his line, with a view to spending the night on the field. His baggage and military chest were sent down to Cockenzie under guard.

Meantime the Jacobite leaders were holding a conference by candlelight. Lord George Murray proposed that they should make a night march still farther to the east and cross the marshes by a path which had been pointed out to him by a local Jacobite sympathizer, Robert Anderson, and so get between Cope and Dunbar and come against him at early dawn from the direction from which he would least expect or desire them. This daring proposal was well received—it had, indeed, a touch of genius in it—and they moved off accordingly a little before 4 A.M.

The Camerons were still in front, and in the ordinary course of things would have formed the extreme right wing when the army emerged upon the plain and faced to the left to move against the enemy. But the Macdonalds had claimed the right wing as the place of honour, and therefore the army 'marched by the left,' so that as it deployed upon the plain the Macdonalds became the right wing, nearest the sea, and the Camerons the left. The Atholl Stuarts had been left behind on the high ground in the hope of deceiving the enemy, and they did not rejoin until just before the attack. Also thirty-six of Charles's fifty horsemen were posted at Tranent, so that they might be conveniently situated to cut off some of the runaways in the event of victory.

But if there was any serious expectation of surprising Cope it was disappointed. It would have been strange indeed if, with his undisputed superiority in cavalry, he had failed to ascertain the movements of his enemies. Finding them now in what had been his rear, right across his former line of march, he swung round once again to

face them, so that the road to Edinburgh was now behind
him. His movements during these preliminary manœuvres remind one of nothing so much as some ponderous
pugilist pivoting slowly on his heels to confront a more
agile opponent. The disposition of his line of battle had
never altered: the guns now on the extreme right, then
Lee's (the 44th) regiment forming the right wing, Guise's
(the 6th) and Lascelles' (the 47th) in the centre, and
Murray's (the 46th) on the left. Gardiner's dragoons
(afterwards the 13th Hussars) and Whitney's squadron
were on the right flank, Hamilton's (14th Hussars) on the
left near the sea. The only hitch that had occurred in
the course of the various turning movements was that
the right wing had become a little bunched, so that
Whitney's dragoons, instead of forming in line with
Gardiner's as had been intended, had to take station in
front of them.

The Highlanders, as they settled into their line in the
darkness, found themselves among fields recently cut for
the harvest and still thick with stubble. There was no
time to rest; dawn was already breaking. They turned
immediately to their left and began to advance towards
the enemy at a kind of cavalry pace, first a walk, then a
trot, then a run. They had apparently advanced too far
towards the sea, and Lord George Murray, realizing
this, ordered them to march half-left. The Atholl men
crossed the marsh at this juncture and fell in behind,
forming the second line.

There was a thick mist at first, but presently it lifted,
showing the two armies to each other at surprisingly close
range. There were no hedgerows or bushes, as nowadays, to interrupt the view. The sight of the red coats
seemed to rouse the Highlanders to fury. As they trotted
forward, says an eyewitness, they might be heard "speaking and muttering in a manner that expressed and

heightened their fierceness and rage." Prince Charlie
was with the Chevalier Johnstone (who has left us a
lively account of the battle) not more than fifty paces
behind the front line. It was a good deal nearer than
he should have been allowed to go, since one stray
bullet through his head must have meant the end of the
Rebellion. He could hear the stubble rustling under
the feet of the Highlanders in the front line as they ran
forward at an ever-increasing pace.

The brief red line of regulars stood looking at them.
They had advanced, as we have seen, obliquely from the
right, in what is technically known as a half-left direction.
Every corporal knows what invariably happens when
such a movement is attempted. The Camerons on the
extreme left found themselves some hundreds of yards
ahead of the rest of the line; and soon they were well
within range of Cope's guns, which were immediately
opposite to them. This was the gunners' opportunity.
But they do not appear to have fired a single shot until
the Camerons came within musket range. Then, hearing
the bullets whistling about their ears, they promptly
dispersed.

A company of Lee's regiment had been appointed as an
'artillery guard' under the orders of Lieutenant-Colonel
Whiteford, and this gallant officer immediately brought
up his men and, rushing forward, fired five of the six
field-pieces with his own hand. Several Highlanders were
hit and the line "seemed to shake," but they kept on
advancing "at a great pace." Whitney's dragoons were
ordered forward. The Camerons stopped in their stride
and began firing at them with their miscellaneous collection of firearms, more suited to a museum than to a field
of battle. "Naked ruffians with uncouth wappons,"
says a contemporary Whig sneeringly. The response of
Whitney's dragoons was to turn right about, ride over

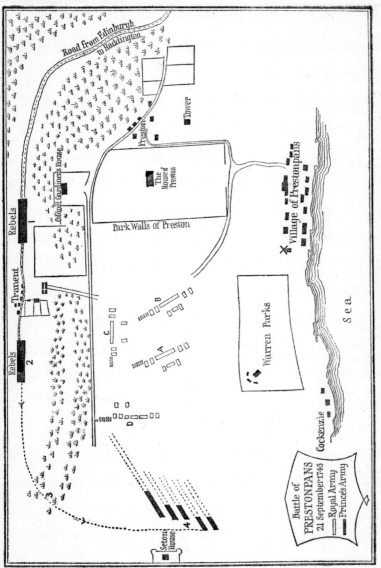

A, B, C, and D are the successive positions taken up by Cope's army; and 1, 2, 3, and 4 show the advance of the Highlanders.

Road from Edinburgh to Haddington

Rebels

Colonel Gardiner's House

Tranent

Rebels

2

Preston

Tower

The House of Preston

Park Walls of Preston

Village of Prestonpans

C

B

A

D

Warren Parks

Cockenzie

Seton House

Sea

Battle of
PRESTONPANS
21 September 1745
Royal Army
Prince's Army

the artillery guard, and gallop away to safety. Gardiner's squadron, after a half-hearted attempt at a charge, followed them.

The Highlanders threw away their muskets. The right flank of Cope's army had gone, but they seem to have made no attempt at envelopment—they simply ran straight on towards the nearest enemy, yelling their Celtic war-cries. But before doing so, says Lumisden (who was present),[1] they "pulled off their bonnets and, looking up to heaven, made a short prayer." Though they had overrun the guns, and the dragoons had fled, it still seemed impossible that they should succeed. There remained the British infantry, the famous scarlet-clad foot-soldiers, whom all the chivalry of Europe could not break, the stolid, tight-lipped men who had turned the tide of battle after battle, from Ramillies to Dettingen. And here was a thin line of half-dressed Highlanders, running towards them across the stubble, with absurd medieval shields in their left hands, waving naked swords in the right. The result could only be a massacre. One or two steady volleys and the battle was done.

What followed never has been, and never can be, explained in military terms. To the regular soldier it might have appeared a miracle if it had not been repeated at Falkirk. There was the cowardly example of the dragoons, of course; the wild stories of the Highlanders' ferocity, eating human flesh and so forth; and there was the fact that Cope's men saw their retreat cut off, with no town to run to except Edinburgh, which was in Jacobite hands. Moreover, most of Cope's infantry, though there were veterans among them, were half-trained recruits; and he had been so tardily supplied with arms and ammunition that there had been small opportunity to train his recruits in the use of their weapons;

---

[1] He was one of Charles's secretaries.

while the cavalry horses, as was common in those days, were so little habituated to the sound of firearms that they were liable to bolt with their riders at any time.

Still, these were regular British infantry, wearing the same glorious uniform that had stemmed the tide at Dettingen in 1743, and in May of this very year had, at Fontenoy, turned a defeat into something like a moral victory. And here they stood silent in their ranks facing that ragged line of leaping, running swordsmen. Who could say what passed through their minds? Army psychology, like mob psychology, is a thing incalculable. Distance from home, an English dislike of the Scottish Whigs, a doubt of the justice of their cause, a mental picture of the rather inadequate figure of poor Cope compared with the gallant lad on the other side, come to claim his own again—all these mice may have been separately gnawing at the fabric of that army's morale.

As the Highlanders drew nearer, the troops began to fire at them without waiting for orders; and since the Camerons, on the left, were still in front, the fire ran down Cope's line from right to left in a half-hearted and ineffectual splutter. And the English line broke too, from right to left, never waiting for the clash of bayonet against basket-hilted sword, but making off at the double for the nearest cover, so that within fifteen minutes of the opening of this extraordinary battle "the whole prospect was filled with runaways and Highlanders pursuing them." By the time that Prince Charles, sword in hand, came up with his own front line he found not an enemy to oppose him. The left wing had crumpled as quickly as the right, and Hamilton's dragoons, who were posted there, had been the first to take to flight. If Charles had possessed any cavalry Cope's losses must have been severe. As it was the fugitives (or most of them) made a wide circuit to the south-east, and eventually reached the gates of Berwick, where their general had already arrived without his army. Hey, Johnnie Cope!

Those of the royal troops who attempted to prolong resistance behind the walls of Colonel Gardiner's estate or in Preston village were quickly rounded up and disarmed, while the baggage guard in Cockenzie, mainly composed of Highlanders of the Whig persuasion, hastened to surrender to the first responsible officer whom they saw.

There were half as many prisoners as there were men in Charlie's army; and as they began to drift along the road or through Prestonpans to Edinburgh, the splendour of their achievement dawned upon the Highlanders, and they danced and cheered like madmen. By the time they had all drifted into Duddingston it was getting dark again, and the Prince once more took up his quarters there for the night.

From Arthur's Seat and the heights above Duddingston that enthusiastic Edinburgh mob (which would do anything for Prince Charlie except fight for him) had listened all day for the sound of battle, had heard its brief clamour, and in the early hours of the 21st of September may even have seen the flash of guns on the plain beyond Prestonpans. And as the sound drew ever nearer, yet not a single Jacobite fugitive appeared, they must have guessed roughly what had happened. They hastened back to the town to make preparations for the proper reception of the victor. Nor is there the slightest reason to doubt that they would have done as much for Cope.

Next morning, which was Sunday, Charles began his return march into Edinburgh. Presbyterian ministers of the type of Patrick Crichton must have watched with dour faces the eager throng of citizens of both sexes pouring through the Canongate to meet him. As the crowd came out upon the hillside they saw the victorious army emerging from the village of Duddingston in parade order, with the Prince and his principal officers on horseback at their head—first the pipers playing (at the Prince's suggestion) *The King shall Enjoy his own Again*; then the clansmen, Macdonalds, Camerons, Stuarts, each regiment under its own chief; then the English prisoners; then the carts with the wounded, English and Scots all mixed together and equally well cared for, but the great majority English. An amazing procession. The cheering crowds lined the roads as they approached, and the people followed the Prince all the way to Holyrood, and stood outside the gates of the palace cheering as they had on the night of his arrival. But at Charles's request the rejoicings were cut short. The killed and wounded on both sides were his own subjects.

Thus ended one of the most surprising skirmishes in British military history. The numbers engaged were almost comically small, and, thanks to the lack of cavalry on the winning side, the casualties were comparatively few. But the psychological effect was tremendous. Coming on top of Spean Bridge and Colt Bridge, it convinced the Highlanders not only that they were superior to their enemy man to man, but that they could get to close quarters with him whenever necessary, in spite of his artillery and small-arm fire. As for the Prince, we have Elcho's word for it that, as the result of Prestonpans, he "entertained a mighty notion of the Highlanders, and ever after imagined that they would beat four times their number of regular troops."

CHAPTER VII

THE MARCH INTO ENGLAND

AMONG the spectators of the battle of Prestonpans was Alexander Carlyle, who, as we have seen, was a moderate Whig in politics. Seeing the day lost for King George, and being himself without arms, he had offered his services to the Prince in order to help with the wounded. He had watched the Highland charge from the high ground above Tranent, and had seen the broad plain suddenly filled with flying redcoats, many of whom fell under the bullets of their pursuers before they could gain cover in the villages. He had come down on to the stricken field, and had been sent into the village of Cockenzie to look for certain medical chests which had gone astray. There, for the first time, this mild, unwarlike Lowland Whig found himself in the midst of the Highland army.

His impressions are interesting. He is no fanatic. He does not, like Crichton, dismiss them all as "caterpillars"—they who could break a British line! But he observes that the men were "in general of low stature, and dirty, and of a contemptible appearance." The officers, on the other hand, were "gentlemanlike" and "very civil." Carlyle probably found them pleasanter fellows to deal with than some of the blustering regular officers on the other side.

But there was one exception. As Carlyle was making for Cockenzie he met "a Highland officer with his train" and was unceremoniously stopped by this officer and commanded with "an air of savage ferocity" to show the way to the nearest inn. The officer was Lord Elcho.

Henderson, the historian, has noted that as Charles first rode into Edinburgh on the 17th he seemed to keep his eye resting a full five minutes on the figure of Elcho, who rode on his left, as though a little doubting this latest recruit (he joined at Edinburgh, as we have seen).

Now, following his return to Holyrood, the Prince appointed a Council of War, consisting of the Duke of Perth, Lord George Murray, Lochiel, Keppoch, Clanranald, Glengarry, Glencoe, Ardshiel, Lord Lewis Gordon (who was doing great things for the Cause in Aberdeenshire and Banff), Sir Thomas Sheridan, Colonel O'Sullivan, Gordon of Glenbucket, Murray of Broughton, and the Lords Ogilvie, Pitsligo, Nairn, and Elcho. This Council met every morning in the Palace, in the Prince's drawing-room. And almost immediately the Prince found himself confronted by two opposing factions—on the one hand Murray of Broughton and the Irishmen (to whom his own sympathies inclined), and on the other hand the Scots. "There was one-third of the Council," says Elcho, "whose principles were that Kings and Princes can never either act or think wrong, so, in consequence, they always confirmed whatever the Prince said." And as the Prince, characteristically, always stated his opinion immediately this made things a little difficult for the other side. According to Elcho, Charles thought of the Highland army as if it were a body of regulars— that is, mercenaries—under his personal command. The Irish adventurers who had followed him from France "had nothing at stake." On the other hand, "the People of Fashion that had their all at stake . . . thought they had a title to know and be consulted in what was for the good of the Cause." Charles is represented as impatient of any kind of criticism and instant to take a dislike to anyone who differed from him on the smallest point.

DAVID, LORD ELCHO
By permission of the Hon. Sir Evan Charteris, K.C.

It is amusing to reflect that among these "People of Fashion" the Duke of Perth and Tullibardine "talked broad Scots" and had difficulty in expressing themselves in English, while many other of the chiefs had seldom, if ever, travelled more than a hundred miles from their ancestral castles. They may have been gentlemen, in the best sense of the word, but they were certainly not particularly fashionable. Elcho himself was one of the few officers in the Prince's army who was in fact a man of fashion. And he was the only one who behaved like a bully at Prestonpans.

The chief question before this Council of War—and, indeed, the only question of major importance—was one of strategy. What was to be the next move? Charles's personal inclinations, backed by many practical considerations, suggested an immediate advance into England, with the object of seizing London before military reinforcements could be brought back from the Continent, where we were, as usual, involved in war with France. Hume has left it on record that "the friends of the Government" were "extremely apprehensive" lest Charles should make this bold stroke. Nothing could have saved the English capital. It sounds absurd, but there is apparently no doubt that these two or three thousand Highlanders, with their amazing marching capacity, could have got to London and occupied it before any superior opposing force arrived from France.

But there were other considerations in Charles's mind. Two thousand Highlanders would almost disappear among the vast population of London (it was bad enough in Edinburgh), nor was he anxious to display the paucity of his numbers in the northern counties of England, where, if he made a brave show, he might hope to gain recruits. Moreover, the news of Prestonpans had got abroad in the Highlands, and his little army was increasing in numbers every day. He determined, therefore, to sit still until he was in a position to lead a respectable force across the Border. He remained in Edinburgh from the 21st of September to the 4th of November.

Holyrood is full of memories of the Forty-five. There may be seen the famous bed on which the young Pretender slept—as also King Charles I before him and the Duke of Cumberland after him! And there, up the stairs to the left as one enters, is the Picture Gallery, in which he held his receptions and balls. It was Charles's custom to sup in public, when there would be music and afterwards dancing. We know that when it came to treading a measure he could hold his own in any company in the world, but Maxwell of Kirkconnel says that on these occasions Charles himself never danced. According to another contemporary, he always wore boots, as though to emphasize the fact that he had come to Edinburgh on sterner business. Nevertheless, his social gifts and his power of pleasing could not be suppressed, and there is abundant evidence of the impression he made as he moved among his guests—it has, indeed, passed into a legend.

The women found him irresistibly attractive, but, as always, he was shy and silent in their company, appearing to prefer the conversation of men. "Yet, which is wonderful, the less he courted them, the faster they followed him," says a Scottish contemporary. Frenchmen understand these matters better: the Marquis d'Eguilles, who arrived about this time from France as Louis's Ambassador to the Jacobite Court, immediately remarked that the women adored Charles "not because he is coquettish or a man of gallantry—quite the contrary: it is because he is not."

To be bashful and tongue-tied among ladies is considered no defect in a modern hero of romance. Mr

Chesterton put our view of it neatly when he remarked that "only one rather cowardly kind of man is not afraid of women." But to the Whig exquisites of the eighteenth century it would no doubt appear ridiculous—especially in a prince. That is probably why Elcho, who disliked Charles, insists that he was "awkward and shy" with the other sex. On the other hand, it is obviously absurd to suppose that a young man of his upbringing and social gifts should have behaved boorishly to anyone. What is certain is that he was as far as ever from that "polite taste for pleasurable vice" which the Duke of Wharton had once urged his tutor to include in the curriculum. In his little Court at Holyrood he was "celebrated for his chastity." And it is interesting to note—before leaving this subject—that he seems to have carried this delicacy with him on the march and to have discouraged the women camp-followers and courtesans who usually swarmed in the rear of eighteenth-century armies. John Daniel, who was with the Jacobites during the retreat from Derby, records how he rescued two female camp-followers who were in danger of drowning as the troops crossed a river. But he adds: "Never an army was known with so few."

Some extraordinary advice was offered to the Prince about this time. The Chevalier Johnstone, for instance, could not see why he wanted to march into England at all. He had recovered Scotland, the ancient kingdom of his ancestors, and "all that he had to do now was to retain possession of it." He should sit tight where he was, strengthen his grip on Scotland, and prepare "to defend himself against the English armies which would not fail to be sent against him." Simple programme! He had only to wait long enough to find himself out-numbered by ten or twenty to one. Yet Johnstone asserts that "this was the advice which every one gave the Prince." If so we can understand his increasing tendency to rely upon his own instinct in matters of broad policy, and to prefer the conversation of the Irish members of his Council, who never offered him advice until they had ascertained in advance that it would be agreeable.

In the meantime, as had been anticipated, his army was steadily increasing in numbers. He held a review of the entire force at Duddingston at the end of October, and found himself already at the head of five thousand foot and about five hundred horse. Several important chiefs had joined him, and the arrival of a few guns from France, added to those captured from Cope, brought the total of his field-pieces up to thirteen. If the French had backed him now with a few battalions of regular infantry and a few squadrons of their famous cavalry it might have made all the difference. Both French and Spanish are accused (on rather doubtful authority) of having made definite promises of immediate help. If so they did nothing to implement them.

There remained only one question to decide—the question of the most convenient route into England. In spite of Johnstone's opinion quoted above, it is clear that by the end of October there was a general agreement among the Jacobite leaders that as soon as their numbers reached a respectable figure they must make a vigorous thrust at London, the capital of Great Britain, rather than allow themselves to be "blotted out" slowly, one by one, as the English veterans from France and the hired foreign mercenaries poured over the frontier.

The strategical problem may be simply stated. There were two roads open—that by Newcastle and that by Carlisle. General Wade would be waiting at Newcastle with a force about equal to the Prince's in numbers. Charles's natural impulse was to go to meet him. The

English could only arrive there two or three days before the Highlanders; they would just have completed their long journey from France, by sea transport and road, and might be expected to be tired. It would be a magnificent thing to brush Wade aside as he had Cope (and how could the Highland charge fail!) and continue his march through the northern counties towards London by this nearest road. England would understand then that this rebellion must be taken seriously. The English Tories would have to show their colours.

This was the view put before his Council of War by the Prince at a fateful meeting in Edinburgh on the 30th of October. Lord George Murray, with most of the Scotsmen, disagreed. He thought that the proposed meeting with Wade was not worth the risk. If they won, their victory would be indecisive; on the other hand, if they lost a battle at this stage the Cause was ruined irretrievably. He proposed to march into England by the way they were least expected—that is, by Carlisle—and, having taken that town, which would be easy, to collect their English adherents there and either march against Wade with augmented numbers or strike southward at London, as they thought best. In order to deceive Wade and give him the slip, Lord George Murray proposed first to march the clansmen as far as Kelso, which was on the Newcastle road, and there halt for twenty-four hours. This would probably tempt Wade out of Newcastle to meet them. Whereupon the Highland army would wheel to the right and get well ahead of him on the road to Carlisle, whither their cannon and heavy baggage would already have been despatched by another route.

This ingenious plan, so characteristic of the supple brain of Lord George Murray, did not at all commend itself to Prince Charles, whose preference was always for the direct attack. However, after hearing the opinions of his counsellors he decided to 'sleep on it' and adjourned the meeting to the following day. Next morning, when they met again, he capitulated so frankly and disarmingly that, according to Murray of Broughton, he "seemed to give great contentment." So the Carlisle plan was adopted.

With thirteen battalions (most of them about the size of a modern company) of foot and rather less than five hundred horse, it was decided to invade England. General Wade was defending with a total force at his disposal of ten battalions, seven of which were composed of foreigners, Germans and Dutchmen. It was a fight between handfuls of Celts and Germans for the soul of a great country which, as they were presently to discover, simply refused to be interested. In Scotland the issue was vital; in England it was never more than a bright topic for the leader-writers and cartoonists, a refreshing little touch of real life in the daily political comedy.

The Highlanders marched out of Edinburgh on the 4th of November and, leaving their pleasant camping ground at Duddingston Park behind them, began their long and momentous march southward. They consisted of the clan regiments of foot, Lochiel, Appin, Clanranald, Keppoch, Glengarry, and the rest, all wearing the Highland garb, so that to the burghers of Carlisle they seemed like so many savages descending upon them from the northern mists.

According to Home,

> the front rank of each regiment consisted of persons who called themselves gentlemen, and were paid one shilling a day; these gentlemen were better armed than the men in the ranks behind them, and had all of them targets [shields], which many of the others had not.

The rather attenuated cavalry consisted of 150 of Lord

Pitsligo's horse, 150 horse guards under Elcho, 130 "horse grenadiers" under Lord Kilmarnock, and 70 "light horse or hussars," whose duty it was to "scour the country and procure intelligence." The pay of a captain in this army was half a crown a day, of a lieutenant two shillings, of an ensign one and six, and of every private soldier sixpence without deduction—a remarkably democratic rate of pay showing much less difference between the emoluments of an officer and a private than exists to-day.

Lord George Murray's plans were so skilfully concealed that by the time he left Kelso, marching by two or three different routes towards Carlisle, the English general had been completely deceived. Not so the Highlanders. For weeks past—ever since they knew that their real destination was England—they had been deserting in scores to go home and help with the getting in of the harvest. Now, as the army marched southward, they began to dribble away again, so that a thousand are said to have deserted before they reached Carlisle, and no captain could be sure how many men he would find under his command when they arrived at the next town. But, though they knew they were for England, their actual destination was so carefully concealed that, according to Johnstone,

hardly any person in our army had the least idea of the place where the junction of the three [sic] columns would take place; and we were very much surprised on finding ourselves all arrive, on the 9th of November, almost at the same instant on a heath in England, about a quarter of a league from the town of Carlisle.

That was good staff work.

From the aged and crumbling walls of Carlisle and from the lofty battlements of the castle the main body of the rebels had been sighted on Sunday, the 10th of November, a thick, foggy day, crossing the river Eden below the town. As they passed round the walls they were fired on by every gun that could be brought to bear, though apparently with little result. They quietly occupied the surrounding villages, erected one or two batteries, and began to make scaling ladders with a view to an assault. Happily for themselves, perhaps, the Highlanders were not to be put to the test of siege warfare.

Carlisle was garrisoned by the Cumberland and Westmorland militia, commanded by Colonel Durand. Though the walls of the city were in disrepair and might easily have been breached, the castle and citadel were still formidable obstacles to an army possessing no siege artillery. Moreover, Colonel Durand must have been aware that the forces being assembled for the defence of the realm were increasing every day, that an army under General Ligonier was advancing on Wade's left towards Lancashire, that a third army was being collected for the defence of London, and that any one of these three outnumbered the Prince's little following.

Yet before the Highlanders had fired a shot against the town—in fact, only two days after their arrival—the defence began to wobble. The militia officers approached Durand with a request that they might be allowed to retreat from the town with their men while there was yet time. He refused, and about four hundred militiamen with some of their officers were got into the castle as a garrison, with ample stocks of food, while an engineer was sent to spike the guns on the city walls.

But a letter came in from Wade holding out no promise of immediate relief, and another from the Prince demanding instant surrender. In reply to a 'feeler' from the Mayor, Charles stated peremptorily:

That he would grant no terms to the town, nor treat about it at all unless the castle was surrendered; likewise if that was done all should have honourable terms; the inhabitants should be protected in their persons and estates, and every one be at liberty to go where they please.

The Mayor, a Mr Pattison, was considerably shaken. He had weakened his personal position by the issue of a foolishly boastful proclamation, in which he declared that Carlisle would hold out indefinitely, and went out of his way to add that he was a true-born Englishman and no relation at all to the Scottish Patersons. Now he sent hurriedly to the castle for the keys of the town, and himself rode out to the village of Brampton to deliver them up to Prince Charles. Whereupon some Jacobite wag composed a poem, highly characteristic of the times, which began as follows:

O Pattison, ohon! ohon!
Thou wonder of a Mayor!
Thou blest thy lot you wert no Scot
And blustered like a player.

The succeeding verses describe Pattison's rather grovelling surrender. On the 15th of November the Duke of Perth took possession of Carlisle in the name of the Prince, the castle also having capitulated on condition that Colonel Durand might be allowed to depart unmolested. Charles made his formal entry two days later. He rode on a white charger, and a hundred Highland pipers played before him.

He was now in a very strong position. Lord George Murray's Carlisle plan had succeeded to perfection. This important town had been captured, and Wade had been left high and dry at Newcastle. There was one danger— that the Duke of Cumberland (who had succeeded Ligonier in command of the second army), advancing from the south, might effect a juncture with Wade, thus forming a combined force more than double the Prince's strength. To prevent this the Prince had only to continue his advance into Lancashire, which must inevitably divert Cumberland's attention, and keep his enemies separated. This bold course was accordingly adopted after a council of war in Carlisle. It was just the sort of plan that appealed to Lord George Murray, who never doubted his ability to give Cumberland the slip, as he had already given it to Wade; and it suited the Prince because it took him a stage nearer to London. There was only one fly in the amber: the English Tories had not risen and showed no signs of doing so. But even in that regard the prospects would be better in Lancashire than at Carlisle.

As soon as the southern advance was decided on Charles sat busily down at his writing-desk, almost like his father in Rome, and began to address letters to his friends on the line of march. To Lord Barrymore, with whom he was personally acquainted, he gave the probable date of his arrival in Barrymore's county, Cheshire, and urged that all sympathizers should be got together by then. He added: "Now is the time, or never." He was always clear on that point—clearer than any of his officers, unfortunately.

Lord George Murray was outwardly rather lukewarm. He had already once handed in his resignation[1] and recalled it; but this further southern march was the logical result of his own ingenious strategy, and once it had been decided on he threw himself into the project with

[1] He was jealous of the Duke of Perth, who, as a Lieutenant-General, was theoretically his equal in rank, under the Prince, and was also more popular both with officers and men. But Perth, who seems to have been a very likeable person, was under no illusion as to his abilities as a soldier. As soon as he heard that Murray had resigned and that Charles had promptly accepted the resignation he joined with the other officers, who were greatly alarmed, in smoothing matters over, declaring that he had no intention of competing for the leadership.

LORD GEORGE MURRAY
From the portrait at Blair Castle
By permission of His Grace the Duke of Atholl 120

his usual enthusiasm. Elcho says that, strategy apart, they would have been compelled to invade Lancashire owing to lack of funds.

They left Carlisle on the 20th of November. The cavalry rode in front under Lords Elcho, Balmerino, Pitsligo, and Kilmarnock. The infantry followed, consisting of the clansmen, Macdonalds, Camerons, Stuarts, Gordons, as before; and now Macgregors, Mackinnons Grants, Robertsons, Maclaughlins, and Macphersons (the last-named led by their chief, Cluny, once the Prince's prisoner and now his ally), and the Lowland regiments commanded by Lord George Murray, the Duke of Perth, Colonel John Roy Stuart, Lord Nairn, and Lord Ogilvie. On the 22nd they were at Penrith, on the 23rd at Kendal, and on the 25th the cavalry had ridden through Lancaster and were at Preston. Preston was the southernmost point reached by the Jacobites in the Fifteen, and as there seems to have been some superstitious feeling in the matter the army was only allowed to remain there one night before pushing on to Wigan.

It had been an amazing march. Every morning the Prince was up early—"first out of bed," says a contemporary—and had personally seen to it that his men were on the march before dawn broke. On one occasion he rode back three miles to bring in stragglers. That active hour before sunrise may have reminded him of his shooting expeditions in Italy—but this was late in November in the north of England! It speaks well for his physical condition that nothing could chill his ardour. Instead of mounting his horse when the columns moved off, he always marched on foot among the clansmen. It does not appear that any of his officers felt equal to following this example! He had also a private carriage of his own, but he made the aged Pitsligo take his place in it all the way. He never ate in the middle of the day, but on reaching his billets for the night would swallow a hurried supper and throw himself fully clothed upon his bed for a few hours' sleep. The wine bills of Charles's headquarters mess happen to have been preserved, and are moderate enough to prove that his staff officers, if they could not equal his marching abilities, were careful to emulate his temperance at table.

As they passed through the hamlets they often found them deserted, but in the larger villages and the towns the people would stand in the doorways staring at them with a not unfriendly curiosity, and now and then a cheer would be raised. The Highland dress was as unfamiliar in Lancashire towns in those days as the costume of an Eskimo would be to-day. The targets and basket-hilted swords had a strangely medieval appearance; no doubt there were Celtic marching songs to listen to. And finally there was the figure of the handsome young Prince, striding past on his way to London. It was difficult not to cheer.

But no one offered to join their ranks. An exception was John Daniel, a middle-aged Lancashire man who has left us his memoirs. This sentimental fellow happened to be on the road "betwixt Lancaster and Garstang" when he saw the "loyal army" pass, "the brave Prince marching on foot at their head." As he looked at Charles from the roadside Daniel felt what he calls "a paternal ardour" fill his veins. Deeply moved, he went into a public-house to think things over. It happened that the Duke of Perth alighted at the same house for refreshment, and, seeing Daniel there, offered him a captaincy if he would join the Prince's army. Daniel agreed, and in a few hours had said good-bye to his family and was at the head of a party of mounted men, scouring the villages for recruits. He managed to collect a handful of thirty-nine new men before they reached Preston. But Daniel was an exception.

"There never was so extraordinary a sort of rebellion," exclaimed Horace Walpole——

> One can't tell what assurances of support they may have from the Jacobites in England, or from the French; but nothing of either sort has yet appeared—and if there does not, never was so desperate an enterprise; ... their money is all gone, and they subsist merely by levying contributions. But, sure, banditti can never conquer a kingdom! On the other hand, what cannot any number of men do who meet no opposition? ... Unless we have more ill-fortune than is conceivable, or the general supineness continues, it is impossible but we must get over this. ... Whatever disaffection there is to the present [royal] family, it plainly does not proceed from love to the other.

No doubt that sums up fairly accurately the general English attitude of indifference. But not every Englishman shared the bovine placidity of the German King, who, whenever the invasion was mentioned to him, answered: "Pho! don't talk to me of that stuff!" In well-informed circles in the city there was great uneasiness, and the alarm in the country districts is well depicted, with what one feels instinctively to be just the right amount of emphasis, in that great novel *Tom Jones*. Even Horace Walpole was presently writing, with an air of flippancy that for once seems a little forced, of letting his beloved London house and flying to the Continent lest he should be caught by "the Pretender's boy." Tories like Smollett said less, but possibly thought the more.

Meantime that gallant little Highland army pressed on southward, deeper and deeper into the heart of England, like a harpoon in the body of a whale. For the first time they were getting some slight encouragement in the matter of recruits. At Manchester, which they reached on the 29th of November, they were even able to form a Manchester regiment consisting entirely of Englishmen.

Here is the Chevalier Johnstone's account of how it happened:

> One of my Serjeants, named Dickson, whom I had enlisted from among the prisoners of war at Gladsmuir [Prestonpans], a young Scotsman, as brave and intrepid as a lion, and very much attached to my interest, informed me, on the 27th, at Preston, that he had been beating up for recruits all day without getting one; and that he was the more chagrined at this, as the other Serjeants had had better success. He therefore came to ask my permission to get a day's march ahead of the army, by setting out immediately for Manchester . . . in order to make sure of some recruits before the arrival of the army. He had quitted Preston in the evening, with his Mistress and my drummer; and having marched all night, he arrived next morning at Manchester, and immediately began to beat up for recruits for the "Yellow-haired Laddie." The populace at first did not interrupt him, conceiving our army to be near the town, but as soon as they knew that it would not arrive till the evening, they surrounded him in a tumultuous manner, with the intention of taking him prisoner, alive or dead. Dickson presented his blunderbuss, which was charged with slugs, threatening to blow out the brains of those who first dared to lay hands on himself or the two who accompanied him; and by turning round continually, facing in all directions, and behaving like a lion, he soon enlarged the circle, which a crowd of people had formed round them. Having continued for some time to manœuvre in this way, those of the inhabitants of Manchester who were attached to the house of Stuart, took arms and flew to the assistance of Dickson . . . so that he soon had five or six hundred men to aid him, who dispersed the crowd in a very short time. Dickson now triumphed in his turn; and putting himself at the head of his followers, he proudly paraded undisturbed the whole day with his drummer, enlisting for my company all who offered themselves. . . .

Such was the origin of the Prince's Manchester regiment. A Colonel Francis Townley, one of the few English gentlemen of the North who had joined the Prince, was put in command. It never exceeded three hundred men, and Johnstone maintained that more than half of these had been collected in advance by that strange recruiting party of a sergeant, his mistress, and the regimental drummer. Nevertheless, there was a distinct and very welcome rise in the temperature as the Highlanders swung into Manchester. The bells of the city rang gaily, and their partisans made a good show at the windows. At night there were bonfires and other illuminations, and the mob stood outside the Prince's lodgings cheering him repeatedly. The Prince, according to Elcho, was so elated that at dinner with his officers he could talk of nothing but what costume he should wear when he got to London, and whether he should enter that city on horse-back or on foot.

In the meantime, though he did not know it, that section of his officers who may be described as the 'defeatists' were holding secret meetings elsewhere, and considering whether to demand a return to Scotland immediately or to wait until they got to Derby. Elcho, explaining their point of view, says that "they did not pretend to put a King upon the throne of England with-out their [the English people's] consent," and that the difficulty they had experienced in recruiting a few hundred "vagabonds" seemed to prove that there was no such consent. However, they decided that they might as well go on to Derby. The Prince might be more amenable by then.

Leaving Manchester on the way to Macclesfield, the army forded the Mersey near Stockport. Lord Stanhope, in his history of the Forty-five, tells a pleasant story of how the young Prince, struggling across the river at the head of his men, found waiting for him on the opposite bank a small group of persons, consisting of some Jacobite gentlemen of Cheshire, and with them a venerable old lady, a Mrs Skyring, a very notable loyalist, who in her childhood had been held up in her mother's arms to witness the return of Charles II to London in 1660. Ever since the expulsion of the Stuarts in 1688 she had annually laid aside one-half of her income and had sent it anonymously to the exiled Court abroad. Hearing of Prince Charles's approach, she had sold her jewels, everything, and had brought the money with her in a purse and now threw it at the Prince's feet as he stepped on shore. Deeply touched—for such loyal gestures had been few— the Prince extended his hand, which the old lady seized and covered with kisses. She survived only a few weeks longer. It is said that the news of the Jacobite retreat into Scotland killed her.

At Macclesfield Lord George Murray got certain news of the whereabouts of that army under the Duke of Cumberland which, as already noted, was advancing against him from the south. The Duke was not, as might have been expected, on his left, but on his right front, quartered at Newcastle-under-Lyme, Stafford, and Lichfield. Since the Prince's objective was Derby, on his *left* front, Murray arranged a little diversion to keep the Duke quiet. Taking the strong, mobile column which was under his own command, he advanced fiercely towards Congleton, drove out a party of dragoons under the Duke of Kingston, and pursued them for some miles along the Newcastle road. Cumberland was completely deceived. Assuming that the Prince was either seeking battle or attempting to break through to the west to join his friends in Wales, he moved his main body to Stone, and there sat still, waiting for the encounter. Lord George in the meantime wheeled sharp to the left and by a forced march got to Ashbourne. Next day, the 4th of December, he entered Derby, with the Prince close at his heels.

CHAPTER VIII

THE FATAL DECISION

A⊤ Derby the usual preparations had been made to receive them. The gates of the town were flung wide open; in every belfry the bell-ropes were industriously, if not enthusiastically, pulled; bonfires were prepared. The municipal authorities hurriedly packed up their civic garments, their chains of office, and so forth, and sent them out of the town, so that there might be no official appearance in their welcome of the Prince. And, having done that, they sat down as calmly as they might to await his arrival.

At eleven o'clock in the morning two horsemen galloped in from the Ashbourne road, and demanded billets for nine thousand men—no less! Mere bluff, of course. "A short while after," says a contemporary account, "the vanguard rode into the town, consisting of about thirty men clothed in blue faced with red, and scarlet waistcoats with gold lace; and being likely men, made a good appearance." They were drawn up in the Market Square, and sat there on horseback for two or three hours, while the air was filled with the sound of the church bells, and the people crowded to their windows to look at them.

Then came Lord Elcho with his life guards, all clothed in the same gay blue uniform, and other chiefs with him, making a fine show as they rode through the streets. The grenadier companies carried on their hats the motto, "A grave or a throne."

Late in the afternoon the clansmen began to arrive, "in tolerable order, six or eight abreast," displaying their standards, white with red crosses, or the gold cross of St Andrew on a blue field, while the pipers played before them as they marched. The Market Square was filled with the white cockades. The magistrates had been ordered to prepare a ceremonial reception for the Prince, but successfully pleaded the absence of their civic robes.

Charles came in at dusk, foot-slogging as usual at the head of his men, and the fittest and keenest among them. Without bothering about receptions he dismissed the parade in the Market Square and went straight to the Earl of Exeter's house, where he was to lodge.

The Highlanders dispersed to their billets, which must have been commodious, since exactly twice as much space had been asked for as was required. But their tastes were simple. Most of them slept on straw—though some had beds—and we have it from several different authorities that after their arduous march they asked for no more elaborate refreshment than a little bread and cheese.

Their attitude towards these fat citizens of Derby, whose wives and property were at their mercy, was almost apologetic in its friendliness. Petty pilfering in their lodgings or in the shops is the worst crime alleged against them; and it is said that occasionally a Highlander would stop some unusually well-shod citizen in the street and compel him to change shoes, very much to his disadvantage. The gravest specific charge against them is that as the vanguard entered the town one of them seized and took away "a very good horse belonging to young Mr Stanford." That was the climax of their wickedness—young Mr Stanford's horse! Generally it may fairly be claimed on their behalf that, unlike many armies, they reserved all their ferocity for the battlefield.

Yet the same English chroniclers who record these facts described the Highlanders as looking like "so many fiends turned out of Hell to ravage the Kingdom, and cut-throats." Their cavalry were "fierce and desperate ruffians." The legend that they were in the habit of eating children was no longer taken seriously perhaps; but when John Daniel reached his billets at Derby he found that the master of the house and his wife had fled, while a trembling housekeeper had all the watches and jewellery laid out ready on the table, hoping thus to avert a massacre of the household staff.

On the other hand, these very same authorities described the Highlanders as

A parcel of shabby, lousy, pitiful-looked fellows, mixed up with old men and boys, dressed in dirty plaids and as dirty shirts, without breeches and wore their stockings made of plaid not much above half-way up their legs, and some without shoes or next to none, and numbers of them so fatigued with their long march that they really commanded our pity more than fear.

Mr Henry Bracken, of Warrington, who saw them march in, reported to the Government in London that they were "a most despicable crew," undersized, "of a wan and meagre countenance," who stumbled along as though hardly able to bear the weight of their weapons. The Prince "looks more of the Polish than of the Scottish breed," and appeared very much dejected. Bracken does not explain how these physical wrecks had so easily outmarched the royal armies, nor how it was that everybody else who saw the Prince at this time found him in a dangerously high state of elation.

It is obvious that the Whig chroniclers cannot have it both ways. There is something unpleasant in their attitude—a mixture of shrill, contemptuous laughter with squeals of fear. One would have thought that ordinary sportsmanship might have extorted from them some word of admiration for this gallant if uncouth little

army of invasion. But even the virtues of the Highlanders were recorded against them. Their Gaelic
speech is described by one Derby householder, who had
some thirty of them quartered on him, as sounding like
the noise of "a herd of Hottentots" or "wild monkeys
... jabbering, screaming, and howling together." What
particularly amused this writer was their habit of saying
grace before meals—"to see such desperadoes pull off
their bonnets and then lift up their eyes in a most solemn
manner and mutter something to themselves by way of
saying grace" was almost too much for his gravity. They
had doffed their bonnets in this same comic way just
before their charge at Prestonpans.

In truth the cheers which they had heard as they
passed through the English villages were for the most
part such as might have been accorded to a travelling
circus. As conquerors they were abhorred. Some old
and deep-rooted racial hatred was here. "In London,"
wrote Horace Walpole, "the aversion to them is amazing."
And he was certainly right in the sense that, whatever
Londoners might think of the dynastic quarrel between
Stuarts and Hanoverians, they loathed the idea of a
Scottish invasion. The news of the occupation of Derby
produced a day of panic in the capital which has gone
down to history under the title of "Black Friday." The
shops were shut; there was a run on the Bank; train-
bands paraded the streets; the Archbishop of Canterbury
composed a special prayer; at Whitehall the Duke of
Newcastle went into his shell and refused to utter a
word, so that there were strong rumours that he was
preparing to go over to the enemy; it was even said that
the King, in spite of his "Pho! pho!" attitude, had a
private yacht waiting at Tower Bridge to carry him to
safety. "No Popery, no arbitrary power!" clamoured
all the newspapers, with a monotonous reiteration of

a single 'slogan' strangely suggestive of our own times.
But though people might agree with the sentiment,
they were not comforted. And the sight of Guardsmen
being publicly flogged in Hyde Park for expressing
Jacobite sentiments was more reassuring to the military
than to the civilian mind. London, in fact, lost its
head.

At Derby, on the morning of the 5th of December,
the Prince, as soon as he had breakfasted, called his
leading officers to a council of war. He was in the best
of spirits—buoyant, confident. As far back as Manchester he had been talking of the manner in which he
should enter London, and now, with Cumberland left
in the lurch, there was no one to bar the way, except
some half-trained militiamen encamped at Finchley and
Highgate. The goal of his life's ambition was in sight at
last. He had made—it must surely be admitted—a
magnificent physical and moral effort to attain it. He
had set an example to the laggards, spurred on the half-
hearted. Who shall say how much of the impetus which
carried that little force in four short weeks from Edinburgh to Derby sprang from the courage, enthusiasm, and
inspiration of their young leader? To him it was now a
mere matter of routine—a choice of the best road to
London. Responding as he always did to the feeling of a
great occasion, he awaited the arrival of his officers in a
mood of exultation.

They came in one by one—Lord George Murray,
Perth, old Pitsligo, Lochiel, Elcho, and the rest. Surely
one glance at their faces must have warned him as they
silently took their seats! There was an air of gloomy
unanimity about them—an unusual thing in itself. The
'defeatist' meeting at Manchester had borne its inevitable
fruit. Charles must have felt the change of atmosphere
and braced himself to meet the shock.

Lord George Murray opened the proceedings in a speech which he himself has briefly summarized for us, and Elcho more fully. He advocated an immediate retreat. He pointed out that, in spite of their successes in action and the ease with which they had marched so far southward, their moral failure in England had been complete. The response to their recruiting appeals had been negligible. They might get to London first, but Cumberland was now reported to be at Stafford, and would follow them close (in point of fact, he was at Lichfield, even nearer). In that event everything would depend on the attitude of the London mob, as to which they had no evidence except what might be gleaned from the apathy of mobs in other towns. "If the mob was against the affair, 4500 men would not make a great figure in London"; and once bottled up in the capital there would be something above thirty thousand regular troops converging upon them from different directions. From Murray's own brief account of his speech it would appear that he argued that they could not, in any case, break through to London. His conclusion was that "they should go back and join their friends in Scotland, and live and die with them."

The Prince sat listening. Through the windows of the council chamber he could hear the sound of high-pitched Gaelic voices in the streets below, as the Highlanders walked about in groups, staring and being stared at. They were in high fettle, these gallant cocks of the North, laughing and singing and talking of London, a city ten times bigger than any they had seen. We have it on record that they were busy sharpening their swords and battle-axes, queueing up for the purpose outside every cutler's shop—instead of picking the lice from their plaids, as their hosts would have preferred. None of them doubted, any more than their Prince had doubted, that London would be the next stop. Charles's eyes softened as he listened. Perhaps he should have ridden among the officers, instead of marching with the men. Then he might have been forewarned.

Lord George Murray's voice droned on. "The Scots have now done all that could be expected of them." What Scots? The officers? The Prince suddenly felt that he himself understood the Highlanders better than their own chiefs. They would follow him! According to Elcho, when Lord George Murray had finished, the other officers present were asked to give their opinions; and all of them, including even Murray of Broughton and the Irishmen (the scene must surely have been pre-pared in advance, their unanimity was so wonderful) agreed with Lord George, excepting only the Duke of Perth and one other, who, perhaps because they had been watching the Prince's face, began to hedge and to say that, instead of flying quite back to Scotland, they might go into Wales and see if the Welshmen would not rise.

The Prince roused himself to answer—though he must have realized by now that an impassable chasm separated him from these men. Elcho says that he "fell into a passion and gave most of the gentlemen that had spoken very abusive language, and said that they had a mind to betray him"—and, indeed, as Andrew Lang has pointed out, in view of the behaviour of Lovat, Boisdale, Macleod, and others, he might well have suspected traitors in the camp. But Lord George Murray, who, though an opponent, was a gentleman, says nothing of this alleged ill-temper, but merely records that the Prince "pressed with all the force of argument to go forward." He further acknowledges that "His Royal Highness had no regard to his own danger." For Charles, after all, had a price on his head, and in the event of defeat was more certain of the scaffold than any of them.

He never gave a thought to that, but kept on urging them to the great adventure. He said he "was hopeful there might be a defection in the enemy's army, and that severalls would declare for him." He "believed firmly that the soldiers of the regulars would never dare fight against him, as he was their true Prince." He seemed to think, says Elcho, who sat there listening with cold contempt, that all the successes he had won were to be attributed "more to men's consciences not allowing them to fight against him, than to the power of the broadsword." (Yet it is hard to explain Prestonpans in ordinary broadsword terms.) He felt so passionately in every fibre that it was, as he had said, a case of "now or never" that it was wonderful that he should have failed to convince them. It seems wonderful—until we remember the most powerful argument of all, never mentioned at the council, which was that when defeat came, if come it must, there would be a better chance of escape in the Scottish heather than in London.

But he moved them. He was pleading for something more than his life. We can believe that his voice shook with emotion. They sat there facing him, thinking of all they had been through together, listening to his eager words, hearing their own clansmen in the street outside cheering the "yellow-haired laddie." Now or never—it was their last chance.

It seems that the Duke of Perth capitulated entirely and went right over to the Prince's side. D'Eguilles, the Frenchman, says that he also agreed heartily with the Prince (but, then, D'Eguilles would not have been a member of the Council). And many others among them must have acknowledged in their secret hearts that the idea of an independent Scotland under a Stuart King was an idle dream, and that the choice they were now taking was between an eventual flight among the Highland hills and a gamble with death in London.

Lord George Murray rallied them again. "I said all that I thought of to persuade the retreat, and indeed the arguments to me seemed unanswerable." Pretty strategist and gallant leader though he was, he craved no martyr's crown, and he knew that there would be short shrift in London for a former official of the Hanoverian Government. Who shall blame him?

The Prince, in his bitterness, thought they were all against him. Many years later, when asked to give his own account of this historic council of war, he wrote that he "could not prevail upon one single person to join with him." He was wrong there, as we have seen. Indeed, when those grave Highland chiefs had left him, filing silently from the room, but glancing back, many of them, to where he sat, lonely and stricken, by the window, a picture of disillusioned heroic youth—from that moment there began to be a very definite reaction in his favour. Tullibardine, who had not been present at the council, was genuinely horrified when he heard of the decision, and it was with difficulty that the leaders talked him round. Others of lesser rank were more obstinate and outspoken in their protests. Lord George Murray himself has told us how, during the afternoon, Sir John Macdonald, one of the original Seven Men of Moidart who had come over with the Prince, sought him out when he was talking to Keppoch and Lochiel, and "railed a great deal about our retreat." "What!" says he to Keppoch, "a Macdonald turn his back!" and to Lochiel, "For shame! A Cameron run away from the enemy—go forward and I'll lead you!" Lord George observes disparagingly that "this gentleman was old, and had dined heartily," and goes on to point out that, holding a commission in the French Army, Macdonald was sure of being treated as a prisoner of war, and could therefore afford to show a braver front than the British subjects, who upon capture were all liable to be hanged as traitors. Still, Macdonald seems to have voiced the opinion of most of the junior officers, not to mention the rank and file.

The Prince sat alone with his misery and his ruined hopes. Only just now a despatch had arrived announcing that eight hundred Irish and Scottish exiles from Dunkirk —picked men from the regiments in the French service— had landed at Montrose and Peterhead, greatly strengthening the Cause in the North. But Lord John Drummond, their commander, carried instructions from Louis XV forbidding him to cross the English Border until all the Scottish fortresses were reduced and his rear made secure. Fatal delay! Also George Kelly, another of the Seven Men of Moidart, who was now in Paris with despatches from Charles to the French Court, wrote cheerfully of much larger reinforcements about to sail, "making you all easy very soon." But Kelly, as though with some prophetic insight, earnestly begged them in the meantime not to retreat: "I wish you may be able to stand your ground, since a *retreat must be fatal.*" That was just the point which the Scottish officers could not, or would not, see. There was still just a chance in London, a gambler's throw. But a retreat could only mean one thing—the failure of the Rebellion.[1]

---

[1] As a matter of fact, there were great preparations in France and Holland in the early part of December. On the 12th Prince Henry, Charles's brother, was at Calais and was received there by the French authorities with royal honours. The English Government's agent wrote characteristically that " he did not see the young man himself to take any notice of him, but has heard from others who did, that he squints." On the 21st Lord John Drummond set up the Jacobite standard at Dundee. But to Charles, sitting alone in that room at Derby, deserted by his friends at the crisis of his fate, all this promise of help was but an added bitterness.

John Murray of Broughton and Sir Thomas Sheridan were announced. They came to say that they had changed their minds. Abjectly they explained that they had only voted for the retreat because it seemed to them that, with the Scottish officers in such a frame of mind, an advance could never succeed. But their hearts were with the Prince. "Some people," says Lord George Murray, "seeing the Prince so much cast down about the retreat, to ingratiate themselves, blamed the resolution." "The little Knave," says Maxwell of Kirkconnel, referring to Murray of Broughton, "argued strenuously for the retreat," until he found it was certain to be carried out, when he pretended to change his mind to please the Prince. Charles probably estimated such support at its true worth. At any rate, he let Lord George Murray know that he withdrew his opposition and that the northern march might begin next day; and he accepted Lord George's offer to command the rearguard in person all the way to Carlisle. (He distrusted him as a politician, but never as a soldier.)

And, having made these decisions, he appears to have sought his own apartments and to have spoken no further with anyone. Nor was he ever again quite the same Prince Charlie who had fired John Daniel's imagination as he marched so gallantly at the head of the clans.

Anyone who has ever marched with the same army in advance and retreat—as so many of us now living have done—must know the dismal, tragic change that comes over the ordered ranks when their backs are turned to the enemy for the first time. There is now no singing, no jokes flashing up and down the column, no whistling of marching tunes, but a grim, *hurt* silence—an unuttered reproach in the sound of those shuffling feet which cuts every officer present to his very soul. He avoids the

137

eyes of the men as they pass him, toiling along the dusty road in their fours, men whom he knows as you can only know men you have fought beside—he avoids their eyes as though he had wounded and betrayed a child. To break the morale of an army, he feels, is to sin against humanity. Above all, he cannot stand their silence. Soldiers only sing when they advance. And is there not something heroic in the spirit of man that makes him sing as he goes to face death and sulk when ordered to retire from it? It is that spirit which is now insulted. There is no silence more eloquent than the silence of an army in retreat.

Just such a change of atmosphere as this might have been observed at Derby on the morning of the 6th of December, 1745, as that gallant little band of Celtic invaders began to pack up their kitbags for retreat. The clansmen were frankly bewildered—stunned. They could not understand it. Here they were within striking distance of London, having brushed aside every opposing force—and now they must retreat! The invasion of England had failed, though not a single military success had been scored against the invaders. "Retreat" was the word—the first retreat of the Forty-five—and retreat from what? They went about their preparations for departure like men in a dream. It was given out that they were only marching north to effect a juncture with the powerful reinforcements from France, now moving south to join them, before Wade could get between; they may or may not have believed this story, but Maxwell of Kirkconnel tells us that "all was sullen and silent that whole day." Their officers were in even worse case. According to a Whig observer, there was an air of panic about them, some of the Highland chiefs even leaving behind them their horses, swords, and pistols in their haste.

But of all the units of that unhappy little army, as it fell into its ranks in the grey light of a December morning for its first march back towards the north, there was none with better cause for uneasiness than the gentlemen of the "Manchester regiment" and the other English volunteers. As the cavalry moved off a certain Mr Morgan, an Englishman, approached a Mr Vaughan, his fellow-countryman, who was riding with the life guards, and the following dialogue took place:

MORGAN. Damn me, Vaughan, they are going to Scotland!
VAUGHAN. Wherever they go, I am determined now I have joined them to go along with them.
MORGAN. By God, I had rather be hanged than go to Scotland to starve!

And so it was. Vaughan got clear away to Scotland. But Morgan—a quarrelsome, eccentric little man—went to London to spy for Prince Charles, and was discovered and duly hanged. On the night before his execution he characteristically disputed his dinner bill with many oaths; and on the very day itself, having ordered specially strong coffee (saying that the prison authorities had never yet given him coffee "fit to come near a gentleman"), he fell into a passion upon finding that it was prepared before he was ready to drink it; and so went fuming to the scaffold.

As the infantry marched out of Derby the cavalry covered their rear. The light horse came last and showed their change of temper by ruthlessly ransacking the surrounding villages for spare horses and arms. Then they followed their comrades. Soon there was nothing but a distant cloud of dust to remind the people of Derby of that odd, brief episode in the history of their town. The "parcel of shabby, lousy, pitiful-looked fellows" had taken themselves off, followed by the mocking laughter of the local Whigs.

As for "their pretended Prince," he emerged suddenly from his lodgings about nine o'clock—when all but the rearguard must have gone—and, having "mounted upon a black horse," he rode rapidly past the marching columns until he reached the van, in company with which he entered the town selected for their next halt. And so he did next day, and the next—nor ever again marched on foot through England with his Highlanders. Daniel, who saw him leaving Derby, thought he looked as though he "wished he had been twenty feet underground."

When the news of the retreat reached London the spirits of the inhabitants went up with a bound. Their behaviour in this hour of triumph was little more edifying than in the panic of Black Friday. There was a noisy outcry for bloody reprisals, now that the danger had passed. "All the world agrees in the fitness of severity to highwaymen," wrote Horace Walpole, "for the sake of the innocent who suffer; then can rigour be ill-placed against banditti, who have so terrified, pillaged, and injured the poor people in Cumberland, Lancashire, Derbyshire, and the counties through which this rebellion has stalked?" He hopes that the Government "will not sow the seeds of future disloyalty by too easily pardoning the present." But then we must remember that Mr Walpole had nearly been compelled to give up his town house!

To Londoners it must have seemed impossible that the Prince's army should again escape. He had "not above 5000 men, if so many." Cumberland was close behind him with 7000 foot (including three battalions of Guards) and 1500 horse—all English. Wade was in front of him with a large mixed force estimated at 14,000 foot and 4000 horse. His infantry had been brought partly from Flanders, partly from Ireland and Holland; 6000 of them were Dutch. His cavalry included the dragoons who had fled from Prestonpans.

But Lord George Murray had deceived Cumberland again—he never found it difficult—by advancing towards him a party of cavalry on the morning of the 6th, when the retreat began. The Duke never realized what was happening until two days later. When he grasped the situation he hurriedly placed himself at the head of his dragoons and 1000 mounted infantry (some say they were mounted behind the dragoons, but this is unlikely) and started in pursuit.

But the duty of intercepting the invaders was obviously not Cumberland's, who had to protect London, but Wade's. Since the beginning of the invasion Wade had done absolutely nothing, except to send Handasyde to reoccupy Edinburgh when Charles evacuated it. He had been too late to save Carlisle, and now, as he once more moved slowly across to the west, it became obvious that he would be late again. His cavalry were at Doncaster on the 8th of December, but when the aged leader himself reached Wakefield on the 10th he saw that by the time he was astride the Highlanders' line of march they must be three or four days ahead of him. He therefore fell back on Newcastle once more, sending on his horse to co-operate with Cumberland's dragoons in harassing the retreat. Wade's second in command, Lord Tyrawly, once summed him up as "infirm both in body and mind, forgetful, irresolute, perplexed, snappish." Even the English Government was getting tired of him now.

But the Highlanders were not really exerting themselves. The old spring had gone out of their step; there were many delays. Lord George Murray complains of the Prince's new trick of rising late, which kept back the rearguard, since they could hardly start without him. He grumbles about the wagons, which were supposed to have been sent on in advance with the heavy guns, and of the general slackness of the staff work at the Prince's

141

headquarters. Yet somehow they continued to out-march their opponents.

At each familiar town on the old line of route the Highland army would receive a formal welcome, more or less perfunctory according to whether the inhabitants believed the prevalent rumour that the Duke had defeated them in battle and that this retreat was really a flight. And as they left by the northern gate they would hear the bells already ringing behind them to welcome the Duke, or perhaps General Oglethorpe with Wade's cavalry.

As they left Manchester a Whig fanatic fired a shot at O'Sullivan, mistaking him for the Prince. No one was hit, and Charles sternly forbade reprisals. Coming into that same town on the previous day, they had found a young soldier of their vanguard lying murdered by the side of the road, and in a cottage near by an old woman and her son with their garments stained with blood. But the Prince would not have these people hanged, since nothing could be proved against them. His magnanimity in such cases was extraordinary. As Andrew Lang remarked, he "made war like a gentleman." It was poorly rewarded. At Congleton, on the march south, Murray's advance guard had captured Weir, the spy, as he tried to escape from a window; but Charles had set him free, and he afterwards became the chief witness against the Jacobites taken at Carlisle, sending many of them to the scaffold.

The effect upon the Highlanders of this change of temper in the countryside was a strong disinclination to be left in the rear. At the beginning of the retreat there had been so many stragglers that Lord George Murray had found it necessary to detail one officer from every battalion to march with the rearguard, and whip up his own men. But now they pressed forward eagerly, and those who were footsore did not hesitate to commandeer any kind of vehicle in sight. Horses were in great demand. Many were taken straight from the plough in the fields by the side of the road, and John Daniel gives us an amusing picture of the Highlanders riding, three or four together, upon the broad backs of these patient animals —"without breeches, saddle, or anything else, but the bare back of the horse to ride on, and for their bridle only a straw rope." "In this manner," he adds, "we marched out of England." He speaks feelingly on the subject. Having been sent in advance with a message from his colonel, he had his own horse stolen while he drank in an inn, and had to trudge miles through the rain before he got an opportunity of stealing another to replace it.

The familiar place-names succeeded each other in the reverse order—Wigan, Preston, Lancaster, Kendal. At Preston the Prince, finding Oglethorpe close on his heels, wanted to halt and make a stand. But it was pointed out to him that Wade might get his infantry to Lancaster, and so bar the way to Scotland, and he therefore agreed to march to that town, which he occupied on the 13th, the same day on which Cumberland reached Wigan. Oglethorpe was in Preston an hour behind the Prince. At supper that night in Lancaster, says Elcho, Charles was loud in his complaints against this hurried and undignified retreat "before the son of an usurper." He insisted that there must be a stand at Lancaster. Wade, he argued, was now definitely left behind. They would have a clear road behind them to Scotland. He had had enough of councils of war ; he would never call one again (he did, though only once), but he interviewed his leading officers and urged upon them the advantages of a successful rearguard action at this stage. They so far agreed with him that a strong defensive position seems actually to have been selected; but on the following morning the Prince changed his mind, and he ordered the retreat to continue to Kendal.

It was at Kendal that Lord George Murray went to the Prince's headquarters after dark. He came to ask that the four-wheeled carts of the commissariat might be changed for two-wheeled, since the former would never get over the rough roads between Kendal and their next halt at Shap. He was also anxious that the men should be provided with a day's ration of bread and cheese, since at Shap there might be nothing for them. We get a sudden glimpse of army life of the period. The Prince had apparently gone to bed; but O'Sullivan was there, and "he had some mountain Malaga which he seemed very fond of and gave me a glass or two of it." He agreed cordially to Murray's request, but while they sat there over the wine, with their legs under the table and their wigs pushed back, time sped on, and Lord George Murray realized that no general orders were being issued, though officers from every regiment in the army were kicking their heels in the outer room, waiting to receive them. He left at 11 P.M. in an irritable frame of mind which the Malaga had failed to soften.

Next morning he had more trouble than ever before with unsuitable carts, stragglers, confusion, and general lack of staff work. Some ammunition wagons broke down, and the rearguard had to spend the whole night on the highroad in the rain. Next day the main body marched on to Penrith, the last stop before Carlisle; but it was as much as the artillery and rearguard could do to struggle into Shap.

It was the last lap of the race, and they had only just won it, for Cumberland, with his dragoons and mounted infantry, was right on top of them at Shap. As Lord George Murray moved out of the town at dawn with his rearguard and the Macdonalds of Glengarry, who had been left behind to assist him, he could see troop after troop of the enemy's light horse on the hills beside the road, riding two and two against the skyline, while the sound of "a prodigious number of trumpets and kettle-drums" broke upon their ears, so that they supposed at first that all Cumberland's army must be there. They halted, irresolute. But a Mr Brown, of Lally's regiment, who was at the head of the column, drew his sword and ran up the hill towards the enemy, followed by his men "as fast as our legs could carry us." Seeing which, Lord George Murray, who was in the rear, unleashed the Macdonalds, and these, outstripping the others, arrived first at the top of the hill, greatly to the consternation of a small body of English light horse, who found themselves mistaken for an army and galloped off in haste. Why they were so over-equipped with kettledrums has never been explained.

The Highlanders resumed their march. But there was more to come. Two miles farther on the Macdonalds in the rear were suddenly charged by a body of Cumberland's cavalry, two thousand strong. Luckily the road was lined by thick hedges and ditches, so that the horsemen could not get round their flanks. The Macdonalds valiantly repulsed the attack with their swords, and then, turning, ran down the road till they overtook the wagons, when they halted, waited for the cavalry, and repulsed them again. Constantly repeating these tactics and, as Johnstone says, "behaving like lions," they came into Clifton, two miles before Penrith, with very little loss.

But the pursuers were increasing in numbers every moment. As Lord George Murray rode into Clifton he could see them drawn up on Clifton Moor, an open plain by the side of the town, the local light horse dressed in green uniforms, Cumberland's dragoons and mounted

infantry in the familiar scarlet. It was clear that a
rearguard action must be fought to shake off these pursuers, and, since Murray's position at Clifton was a strong
one, the Prince at Penrith sent back the Macphersons,
the Stuarts of Appin, and Colonel Roy Stuart's Lowland
regiment to support him. There followed a curious
scrambling engagement. The country, as we have seen,
was much broken up by hedges and ditches—a thing less
usual then than now—so that the English cavalry could
not get at their opponents without dismounting. This is
what five hundred of them proceeded to do, and, leaving
their horses in the open plain, advanced in skirmishing
order from ditch to ditch and hedge to hedge, keeping
up an irregular fire. Roy Stuart's regiment was astride
the road, the Appin men lined the hedges on his left,
with Cluny's Macphersons beyond them, and the Glengarry Macdonalds were on the right of the road. Lord
George Murray allowed the enemy to creep closer and
closer, gaining confidence from the superiority of their
fire, and then suddenly launched his attack. By this
time the light had faded, and the dragoons could scarcely
see the sights on their muskets when a succession of wild
yells, coming from both sides of the road, warned them
of a Highland charge. Jumping the hedges, swords held
high in the air, the Highlanders were on top of them in a
moment: many a good broadsword was ruined that day,
says Johnstone, by violent contact with the dragoons'
steel skull-caps. The dragoons were quickly driven back
on to the open moor, while the Highlanders resumed
their former position behind the hedges.

A few hours later Lord George Murray, having got all
his baggage and artillery safely on its way to Carlisle,
quietly withdrew his men and marched north in the darkness to join the Prince at Penrith. But since the enemy
were now so close at their heels they made no stop at

Penrith, but pushed on to Carlisle, which they reached on the following day, the 19th of December.

It was just short of a month by one day since they had marched out of that town to the invasion of Lancashire.

CHAPTER IX

GLASGOW—AND CLEMENTINA

It happened that the day after his arrival at Carlisle—the 20th of December[1]—was the Prince's birthday. There was a sudden uplift—one of those swift psychological changes which may frequently be observed in an army on the march. Whether it was the date or the tonic of that successful charge at Clifton or just the natural resilience and high spirits of youth—whatever the cause —the Prince seemed suddenly to sit up again and take the reins. And that curiously close affinity between Charles and his Highlanders caused an immediate corresponding reaction in the army.

The first result was unfortunate. Full of eager optimism, he sent for his principal officers and consulted them separately—no more conferences!—as to the advisability of garrisoning Carlisle. He must have a jumping-off place for his next invasion of England, when he returned to renew the attack—a date not so far off now, for he had just got news of the landing of French reinforcements in Aberdeen, with siege artillery and engineers. Apparently his officers agreed. It is not even certain that the proposal came first from the Prince. A month afterwards Lord George Murray tried to throw the whole blame upon him; but Charles was able to retort that Murray himself had offered to remain in Carlisle and take command there. A much more foolish charge against him was that of having deliberately sacrificed the Englishmen of the Manchester regiment by leaving them

[1] This is Old Style. By modern reckoning, as already noted, he was born on New Year's Eve.

148

behind—out of spite, it was said, because he was disgusted at the poor response to his recruiting appeals in England. Of less than four hundred men all told in the Carlisle garrison 256 were Scots, including the Governor, John Hamilton. Yet it is certain that Carlisle should never have been garrisoned. It was throwing good men away.

The Jacobite army left Carlisle on the evening of the Prince's birthday, and pushed on towards the north. Coming to the river Esk, they forded it in gallant style, a hundred men abreast, though the water rose to their shoulders. But, as Lord George Murray remarks, "Highlanders will pass a water where horses will not." Some of the men held their clothes above their heads to keep them dry; and all of them danced naked on the farther bank to dry themselves, while the pipers played a reel. Certain gaily dressed Jacobite ladies on horseback had preceded the army across the ford. A few other 'ladies,' as we have seen from John Daniel,[1] were following afoot (and were nearly drowned in the crossing), but these would not be strict in their ideas about sun-bathing. The Duke of Perth re-entered the water several times to bring out exhausted men. Charles, with some of his cavalry, had ridden across a little below the ford. Before he reached the bank he caught sight of two or three of the infantry who had lost their footing and were being swept down stream towards him. "With great intrepidity and presence of mind," says Lord Mahon, who tells the story,[2] "Charles sprang forward and caught one poor soldier by the hair, at the same time calling out in Gaelic, '*Cobhear, cobhear*,' that is, 'Help, help!' and supporting him until he could receive assistance." After reaching the bank Charles, according to Daniel, "suffered a poor soldier, much fatigued, to repose himself in the

[1] P. 113.
[2] In *The Forty-five* (1851). He does not give his authority.

149

King's chair, which till then had been death for anyone but himself to sit in." He brought yet another man to shore seated behind him on his horse. These stories may be apocryphal, but they indicate the Prince's solicitude for his "poor soldiers," which, as Mahon says—and we can believe it—added greatly to his popularity.

After crossing the Esk the army divided, Lord George Murray with the Lowland regiments turning off to the right to make a feint at Edinburgh (he was to rejoin later), while the Prince, with the clansmen, marched direct upon Glasgow through Dumfries, Drumlanrig, Douglas, and Hamilton. They were now among the Whig strong-holds of Lowland Scotland. In many respects it was a change for the worse. If the commons of England had given them poor support they had not been actively hostile. But the good-natured, half-contemptuous, yet admiring cheers of the English crowds as the young adventurer and his troupe went marching through their towns gave place now to black looks and a bitter, eloquent silence. Passers-by averted their eyes; black-coated Presbyterian ministers glared balefully as they passed. It must be remembered that all the Lowlands had been fed with Hanoverian propaganda about an alleged rout of the Prince's army at Lancaster. "The ribals," wrote Bailie Allan to Provost Cochrane, of Glasgow, "are killed, and brok, and taken." Some poor remnant was said to have escaped into Wales. Yet here they were, back in Scotland, still with their tails up! Disappointment did not sweeten the sour visages of the local Whigs.

They entered Dumfries on the 21st. "And extra-ordinary it was," says Daniel, "to see the army, notwith-standing all their fatigue, come in as merry and gay as if they had only marched that morning." What was their disgust as they passed through the empty streets to find "the candles still in the windows" and the bonfires still

MAP OF SCOTLAND

burning in celebration of their supposed defeat! More-over, it was a party of townsmen from Dumfries who had cut off a Jacobite baggage train last November when the invasion of England was begun. Charles now fined the town £2000, and when they could produce only £1100 seized two of the leading Whigs and took them with him as hostages for the balance.

In such circumstances the Highlanders would have been more than human if their attitude towards the civilian population had remained entirely beyond reproach. Even Elcho admits that, approaching Glasgow, they "plundered a little." He mentions Penrith and Lesmahagow—both of them places where Jacobite sympathizers had been arrested and sent prisoner to Edinburgh as soon as the Prince's back was turned. The Whigs made the most of such incidents. The *London Gazette* for the 4th of January, 1746, in a message from its Glasgow corre-spondent, accused the Highlanders of "plundering and burning in a most unheard of manner." On the other hand, Provost Cochrane, Glasgow's leading Whig citizen, wrote on that very same day that the invaders "behaved pretty civilly." Shortly before the Prince entered Glasgow Cochrane's friend William Crosse had written to him reassuringly: "The worst it can come to is breaking your looking-glasses and china: for plundering or burning you need be in no pain." In fact, he suffered no damage at all—or we should have heard about it.

At Hamilton, just outside Glasgow, the army halted, and the Prince deliberately took a day off and went shoot-ing in Hamilton Park. It was the first time that he had been able to indulge in his favourite sport, and perhaps almost the first day free from anxiety, since he had left behind him the blue skies and orange-trees of Italy. We cannot doubt that he often thought of those before-breakfast expeditions of his in search of quail as he carried his gun in Hamilton Park. We do know (from Daniel) that "he behaved to the admiration and surprise of all present, killing or hitting everything he shot at, so that, without flattery, he was looked upon to be the best marksman in the Army." And we know that Mr Gibb, his Master of the Household, thought that he ought to have used this day to snatch a little rest!

"One of the prettiest, but most whiggish towns in all Scotland"—Glasgow—now lay at their feet. It was quite helpless, for the regiment which it had raised locally for the Hanoverian cause had been promptly ordered away to assist in the defence of Edinburgh. "We are 30,000 souls in city and suburbs," wrote the Provost proudly, "with scarce a Jacobite among us belonging to our corporation; not twenty who can so much as be suspected, and these mostly ladies from the country casually residing here." The ragged Highlanders must have looked at those comfortable roofs and lofty spires, framed in green meadows, with hatred and triumph in their hearts. Charles, in fact, had used the pause at Hamilton to send in Hay of Restalrig, who had interviewed the city fathers and told them, roughly enough, that the price of peace was the lump sum of £5000 and a supply of goods and clothing, the latter to consist of "6000 short cloth coats, 12,000 linen shirts, 6000 pairs of shoes and the like number of pairs of tartan hose and blue bonnets." To be forced to manufacture the Jacobite blue bonnets was a bitter pill for Glasgow. It was swallowed, however, and Charles prepared to make a peaceful entry.

He went in on foot at the head of his clans in the old manner. There is general agreement that the streets were crowded, the people standing five or six deep on either side—*and uttering not a sound*. It must have been a curious scene. When the Prince had dismissed his

OLD GLASGOW

From a print in the possession of the Corporation of Glasgow
By permission of the Director of the Glasgow Art Gallery

154

men and was going to his lodgings the Highlanders, says Cochrane, "attempted to huzza two or three times, but fell through it, our mob with great steadiness declining to join in." When Charles was leaving Glasgow a week later he summed up his impression of the place with the remark "that it was indeed a fine town, but he had no friends in it, and what was worse, they were at no pains to hide it from him."

In the meantime, however, he was anxious to please. He was lodged at the palatial mansion (its site now covered by the Trongate) of a Mr Glassford, who had made his fortune "in the Colonial trade," like many others in Glasgow about that time. He kept open house, dining in public every day, and, according to Elcho, "there was always a great deal of company came to see him." We have Gibb's household accounts for this period, and, in view of the later stories about the Prince's drinking habits, it is worth recording that no wines or spirits were ordered, and only four gallons of ale, during the whole seven or eight days' stay; so that, unless Mr Glassford had left a well-stocked cellar, some of the guests must have gone thirsty. But all the accounts of the march from Carlisle show the same moderation. Food, on the other hand, and especially poultry, was in profusion.

The Prince determined to hold a review of his troops for the edification of Glasgow. They were drawn up on the Green, 3600 foot (some of them unarmed) and about 500 horse. A mere handful! In Lancashire and Derbyshire he had been careful to conceal the paucity of his numbers; but now, as a contemporary authority[1] points out, hearing of the arrival of the French and the assembling of the clansmen in the North and "thinking himself sure of doubling his army in a few days," he was "not unwilling to let the world see with

[1] Maxwell of Kirkconnel.

what a handful of men he had penetrated so far into England." So he rode through the streets to the parade ground, dressed "in the French dress," and no doubt looking at his youthful best. One who was a spectator on that occasion writes:

> Like other young people, I was extremely anxious to see Prince Charlie, and for that purpose stationed myself in the Trongate where it was reported he would pass. He was holding a muster of his troops in the Green; and when it was over he passed on horseback at the head of his men on his way to his headquarters. I managed to get so near him that I could have touched him with my hand; and the impression which his appearance made upon my mind shall never fade from it as long as I live. He had a princely aspect; and its interest was much deepened by the dejection that appeared in his pale countenance and downcast eye. He evidently wanted confidence in his own cause, and seemed to have a melancholy foreboding of that disastrous issue which ruined the hopes of his family for ever. [1]

His reception in the streets of Glasgow would have been enough in itself to have damped any man's spirits. According to Cochrane, he showed himself in public four or five times without getting a single cheer or so much as the doffing of a cap by the meanest inhabitant. "Our very ladys had not the curiosity to go near him, and declined going to a ball held by his chiefs: very few were at the windows when he made his appearance, and such as were declared him not handsome." As to the attitude of the "ladys," however, there is considerable doubt. It is curious, and a little suspicious, to find every Whig historian harping upon this point. They protest too much—so that the relations of this young misogynist with the opposite sex get more space than those of any lady-killing hero in history. Daniel, who was with the Prince, after describing the grace and dignity with which

[1] From *The Cochrane Correspondence* (Glasgow, 1836),

he rode through the ranks at the review and the "multi-tudes of people who had come from all parts to see us," adds that "especially the ladies, who before were much against us, were now, charmed at the sight of the Prince, become most loyal."

One lady must be mentioned particularly. There is no certain proof that she was actually introduced to the Prince at Glasgow. It may be that they first became friends a few days later at Bannockburn, where they were fellow-guests in her uncle's house. That is Elcho's state-ment, but Elcho hated the Prince and is an unsound guide. She was Clementina Walkinshaw, one of the Walkinshaws of Barrowfield; her father had a house, Shawfield, in Glasgow, and it seems only reasonable to assume, in view of the strong Jacobite tradition of her family, that she would be one of those "ladies from the country casually residing here," referred to by Cochrane (p. 154), who annoyed the good Provost by openly wearing the white cockade. If she did meet the Prince in Glasgow they would have plenty to talk about. It is one of the prettiest coincidences in the Young Pretender's romantic contribution to history that his eye should have been caught by this young girl, whose father had helped the Chevalier Wogan in the preliminary arrangements for the rescue of her namesake, his mother, from Austria.[1] I think that they must have had many conversations at the Glassford mansion in Glasgow, and that it was here that he obtained from her—the first woman who had entered his life—"a promise to follow him wherever Providence might lead, if he failed in his attempt." Possibly the promise was sealed at Bannockburn, or, as Elcho coarsely puts it, that she "forthwith became his mistress" there. We shall see later how poor Clementina kept her word.

It is a damning confession for a biographer to make

[1] Walkinshaw was the Jacobite agent at Vienna at that time.

nowadays, but the truth is that women played only a secondary part in the life of this frustrated man of action. It is tempting to suggest that Charles's "pale countenance and downcast eye," while at Glasgow, were due to the agitation of his heart over this first love affair. But the fact is that he had more than enough to worry him in the affairs of the outside world. It was at Glasgow that he heard of the fall of Carlisle before Cumberland's heavy artillery. The garrison had been compelled to surrender to the King's mercy. The Englishman, Colonel Townley, in command of the Manchester regiment, and John Hamilton and the other officers were sent to London to stand their trial. Nine of them were executed, and for a long time afterwards poor Townley's head remained exposed upon Temple Bar, in Fleet Street, where it must have been observed with disgust by that eminent Tory Samuel Johnson, who in those days was often reduced to roaming the streets at night without sufficient money to pay for his lodgings.[1]

But it was at Glasgow, we are told, that the Prince finally abandoned the idea of renewing his invasion of England. What more need be said? He had recovered his spirits now, and would play out the game to the end, like the sportsman that he was. But this was the death of his high hopes, the grave of his ambition, and he must have known it. This rang the curtain down on the great adventure of his life, and all that remained, so it must have seemed to him—though, in fact, he was wrong—was in the nature of an anticlimax.

This was the second of the three fatal decisions of the Forty-five (the first was at Derby). Now, for the second time, the dictates of caution prevailed. It was not the

---

[1] It has been suggested that Dr Johnson was out with the Jacobites in the Forty-five; and it is true that he seems to have published no literary work of importance in 1745 and 1746. But the *Dictionary* may have been in preparation.

Prince's decision—it was forced upon him. With the numbers under his command it would have been sheer madness to march south again. But the amazing and tragic fact is that only sixty miles to the north, at Perth, ample reinforcements were waiting for him—and went on waiting! There was Lord John Drummond, with some of the Frenchmen just landed; there was a fine rally of the clans—probably four thousand men in all. The Prince had sent urgent orders from Dumfries for these fresh troops to join him at Glasgow. They did not do so. Lord John Drummond, as we have seen, was handicapped by over-cautious instructions from the French Court, and the fatal decision was probably his. At any rate, the Prince never got his succours, and all chance of saving Carlisle and renewing the invasion of England was lost.

Otherwise the news was good. There had been great doings in the north. Lord Lewis Gordon was Lord-Lieutenant of Aberdeenshire, and he had carried the whole county for the Prince. In his official capacity he had raised three battalions of Lowlanders from the parts of the country towards the coast, mostly by the simple process of compelling every landowner to furnish so many men. His levies seem to have served willingly enough; though the Rev. Mr Bisset, a Presbyterian Whig, records that, during the Jacobite recruiting in Aberdeen, "I am ravished to hear that when the drum beats not a few of the boys cry, 'God save King George!'" At the same time the dribble of French reinforcements had begun to arrive at Aberdeen and Peterhead.

The Whigs of Aberdeen looked round for help. General Handasyde at Edinburgh was too far away, so they sent urgent messages to Lord Loudoun, who was holding Inverness for the King. But Lord Loudoun had his own difficulties. As a glance at the map will show, he occupied an isolated position almost surrounded by hostile clans; and a great assemblage of Jacobite clansmen was taking place to the south of him, at Perth—Mackintoshes and Farquharsons and Frasers, with Macdonalds and Stuarts and Camerons who had been too late to join the Prince in his march south. All through the Highlands there was a new glow of enthusiasm for the Prince's cause. Mackintosh and Seaforth personally had sided with the Government, and were actually with Loudoun in Inverness; but their wives thought otherwise. Lady Mackintosh raised the clan in her husband's absence and sent it to join Drummond at Perth; Lady Seaforth did the same. Loudoun had with him that remarkably able man Duncan Forbes, Lord President of the Session, whose idea it had been to make Inverness a Hanoverian rallying-point in the North. He had also succeeded in securing the person of the wily old Lord Lovat, head of the Frasers, who, as usual, was trying to hunt with the hounds and run with the fox. But Lovat had just slipped away and gone back to the hills. And Lovat's eldest son had already led the Frasers south to join the Prince.

However, Loudoun detached about seven hundred of the "well-affected" clansmen, consisting mainly of Macleods and Monroes (commanded by the Laird of Macleod and Captain Monroe at Culcarin) and sent them forward towards Aberdeen, with a vague idea of at any rate checking Lord Lewis Gordon's recruiting activities. It was a weak move. Lord Lewis promptly assembled his Lowland regiments, with the Frenchmen who had landed at Aberdeen, and marched out to meet the invaders. These Government Highlanders, the Macleods and Monroes, advancing in the casual Highland way, had got as far as Inverurie and halted for a few days' rest, quartering themselves comfortably among the surrounding farmhouses. There were a few posts in

Inverurie itself, but most of the men were in billets well to the rear of the town.

On the afternoon of the 23rd of December one of the outposts "was surprised with the white flag [that is, the Jacobite flag] turning the fir park of Keith Hall in forward march upon the village." He fired his piece to give the alarm. Lord Lewis Gordon was advancing upon both sides of the Don, his Aberdeen regiments on the eastern bank, the Frenchmen on the west. Each column had, therefore, to ford a stream in full view of the enemy (the Frenchmen the Don, Lord Lewis the Urie) before they could get into the village. This was a God-sent opportunity for the Whigs, and such of the Macleods as could be assembled in time opened a brisk fire and killed a few men in the water. But the invaders were quickly across, and, being drawn up in their ranks, marched into Inverurie from two sides, the French firing regular volleys down the narrow streets. The Macleods soon gave way and fled through the fields to the north of the town. On a rumour that Macleod himself had been taken they attempted to rally, but were dispersed by a few well-directed volleys. According to a local Whig minister (who wrote an account of the affair about a year later), their losses would have been much heavier, but, night coming on, the pursuers mistook a furrowed ridge in the "stubble-ground" for a row of men, and wasted precious time shooting at it. Lord Lewis after this victory marched south to join the Jacobites at Perth.

The skirmish at Inverurie, insignificant in itself, is of interest because of its extraordinary reversal of form. When the Highlanders fought for the Prince they were irresistible. When they fought on the Government side they were easily routed by two or three Lowland regiments and a few foreign regulars. Well might Prince

Charles feel himself confirmed in the idea that no troops, Scottish or English, would fight whole-heartedly against their lawful Prince! Put at its very lowest, Inverurie showed that the moral advantage was still with the Stuart cause. It must not be forgotten that up to this moment in the history of the rebellion the Jacobite arms have not suffered a check worth recording anywhere.

The fall of Carlisle, though disastrous in itself, had the advantage of simplifying the strategical situation. Since it was no longer possible to invade England a second time, the obvious move was to effect a junction with the Jacobites at Perth (now under the sole command of Lord John Drummond) as speedily as possible. The united force, which must then amount to eight or nine thousand men, might even be strong enough to recover Edinburgh, where General Hawley had succeeded Handasyde in command (the Duke of Cumberland having been ordered south to meet a possible French invasion). But the most convenient meeting-place between Perth and Glasgow was Stirling; and it was therefore decided to effect a junction there, and to begin operations by reducing Stirling Castle, a task to which the newly landed French artillery was reported to be fully equal.

The Prince's army therefore marched out of Glasgow, in two columns, on the morning of the 3rd of January, with their drums beating and their flags flying. They were in excellent fettle. It must be remembered that the whole invasion of England had cost the Prince in killed and missing only forty men. It had been an exhausting march, but the rank and file felt that they had shared in a great experience. The right-hand column, which was commanded by Lord George Murray, diverged somewhat to the south, passing through Cumbernauld. Their leader, in fact, was making a characteristic

CLEMENTINA WALKINSHAW
Scottish National Portrait Gallery
Photo Annan, Glasgow 162

feint at Edinburgh with the object of 'tying down' the garrison there—quite unnecessarily, as it turned out, for Hawley was waiting for a reinforcement of ten battalions from Newcastle and had no intention of moving before they arrived. The Prince, with the northern column, passed through Kilsyth, where he spent the night, and so on towards Stirling. The junction with Drummond and Lord Lewis Gordon was duly effected, and Charles found himself at the head of by far the strongest force that had yet been under his command.

Some delay followed. The Hanoverians had sent two sloops-of-war from Leith, and their commander, Gossett, sailing boldly up the Forth, succeeded in obstructing the passage of the artillery across the river. Until it was all across the siege of Stirling could not be begun.

The Prince had taken up his quarters in Sir Hugh Paterson's house at Bannockburn. Miss Walkinshaw, Paterson's niece, was his fellow-guest. It is said that he had contracted a feverish chill and that she nursed him. Clementina was not a beauty, unless her portrait lies, nor, so far as we can judge, a wit. But then Charles was peculiarly insensitive to feminine charms. Her face, at any rate, shows animation. She had been born in Rome, and christened there. She was named after his own mother, who had stood sponsor. No doubt these two often talked together of Italy. And then he must catch a cold!

Again, however—and as emphatically as before—he had other things to think about. There was more trouble with his officers. On the second day after his arrival at Bannockburn Lord George Murray presented him with a lengthy protest which had been unanimously approved after a meeting of the leading chieftains. It was the old question of the calling of councils of war. It was said that he never consulted anyone except Murray of Broughton and Sir Thomas Sheridan. If he had called a council at Lancaster they would not have lost a day there; at Carlisle, they would not have left that unfortunate garrison behind; as for Derby, "had not the Council determined the retreat from Derby what a catastrophe might have followed in two or three days!" Finally there was a broad hint that his army consisted of volunteers, not mercenaries, and that he ought to be more careful of their lives on that account.

Stung to indignation, the young Prince bestirred himself—presumably from his sick-bed—to indite a slashing reply. He reminded Lord George Murray that at Lancaster he (Murray) had been in favour of halting not one day, as was done, but two; and that at Carlisle he had himself proposed to remain in command of the garrison. Derby he did not mention, but every one knew his opinion of that wretched decision. On the general question of taking advice he asserted that since leaving Derby he had continually consulted Lord George Murray and others, and that he meant to go on doing so. But, as for councils,

> I came vested with all the authority the King could give me, one chief part of which is the command of his armies, and now I am required to give this up to fifteen or sixteen persons. . . . By the majority of these all things are to be determined, and nothing left to me but the honour of being present at their debates. This, I am told, is the method of all armies, and this I flatly deny; nor do I believe it to be the method of any one army in the world. . . . It can be no army at all where there is no general.

On the question of risking men's lives he points out that he himself is the only one among them with a price on his head. And finally, to sum the matter up: "My authority may be taken from me by violence, but I shall never resign it like an idiot."

164

Rather petulant, no doubt, but excusable in the circumstances. And, having sent Lord George Murray away with a flea in his ear, the Prince sank back upon his pillow.

His respite was to be a short one.

CHAPTER X

THE ROUT OF FALKIRK

IT is comical, and to English readers not a little humiliating, to contemplate the list of blustering, incompetent commanders—scarlet-faced, red-coated bullies of the sergeant-major type—who were sent north one after another with mixed forces of mercenaries, English and German, to endeavour to make head against Prince Charlie's mobile little army, guided by that cunning strategist Lord George Murray. Cope, Wade, Hawley, Cumberland—they all floundered helplessly. Old Wade avoided defeat by the simple process of doing nothing. Cumberland won the only English victory in the Forty-five, and that almost in spite of himself.

General Henry Hawley, who now commanded the royal army in Edinburgh, seemed to embody in his own person all the vices and stupidities of his class. He was a fierce disciplinarian, while at the same time "his beastly ignorance and negligence" were matter of common comment among his own men. Wolfe, afterwards the hero of Quebec, who was his brigade-major at this time, wrote privately to a friend that "the troops dread his severity, hate the man, and hold his military knowledge in contempt." Indeed, he seems to have had only one single idea for this Scottish campaign, which was that the Highland clansmen would never stand up to a charge of regular cavalry—though how he could reconcile such a theory with the results of Prestonpans and Clifton passes understanding.

To the Whig exquisites of St James's and Pall Mall

Hawley was an infinitely more ridiculous figure than the Jacobite "boy" Prince whom they affected to despise. Horace Walpole loved telling stories against him. Hawley, it seems, would hang a man as soon as look at him. The soldiers nicknamed him "Lord Chief Justice" from his "frequent and sudden executions." When a Dutch gentleman called upon him to offer the usual eighteenth-century bribe Hawley seized his visitor by the scruff of the neck, dragged him into the passage, and kicked him downstairs. In fact, he had "no small bias to the brutal." When Hawley died in 1759 he left a characteristic will, full of disparaging references to the legatees: "I writ it all with my own hand," he says, "because I have the worst opinion of all members of the law." The Church was not so easy to dodge: "The priest, I conclude, will have his fee; let the puppy have it." Also, "pay the carpenter for the carcase box." An unpleasant, honest beast.

In the meantime, as we have seen, he had been waiting in Edinburgh for a reinforcement of ten battalions from the south. He used the interval to erect gibbets in the streets for the public execution of his prisoners after victory had been won, and, in order to save time, he appointed certain hangmen to accompany his army on its march. Having completed these arrangements and having received his reinforcements, he marched out of Edinburgh, full of confidence and athirst for blood.

The Jacobites were about to begin the siege of Stirling Castle. The town had surrendered at discretion, but the English troops, under that stout soldier General Blakeney, had retired into the castle and were preparing to defend themselves. The French siege artillery had only just arrived (on the 14th of January) when news was brought to the Prince that General Hawley was advancing and was already in the neighbourhood of Falkirk. On the

16th he was reported to be encamped a little to the north of that town, which some of his infantry had occupied. He had been joined by about a thousand Campbells. The situation was critical. Lord George Murray thereupon produced one of his ingenious schemes. He suggested that the army should march by Torwood, encircle the town of Falkirk, and gain the high ground to the south of the town before the enemy could prevent them. They would thus appear to threaten Hawley's communications with Edinburgh, and force him to attack them at a disadvantage. Lord George said that he knew the ground and proposed to lead the column himself on foot. The Prince enthusiastically agreed—as he did to all Murray's plans except when they involved retreat.

Accordingly, about noon on the 17th of January the Jacobite army was drawn up in two long lines as though for an ordinary inspection. In the front rank, composed of Highlanders, the Macdonalds were on the right, the Camerons, Gordons, and Stuarts on the left. The rear rank was composed of the Lowland regiments, under Lord Lewis Gordon, with the Atholl brigade on the right. The cavalry, with Lord John Drummond's Frenchmen,[1] were behind the rear rank. But, instead of inspecting them, Prince Charles gave the simple order: "Right turn!" and marched them off in columns of clans towards the south, the Macdonalds leading.

Now, it is hard for the modern mind to understand the extraordinary difficulty of handling such an army as this was. They could not be deployed on the field of battle in the manner of regular troops. To give a company of Highlanders such an order as "On the right (or left) form company" meant instantaneous confusion

---

[1] The men brought over from France by Drummond consisted of his own French regiment, the Royal Scots, and the Irish " pickets "—*i.e.*, fifty men picked from each of the six Irish regiments in the French service. The total was about eight hundred. There were also some cavalry landed.

and delay. The Chevalier de Johnstone, who served with the Prince's army and was present at Falkirk, gives an interesting account of how this difficulty was got over. It was the practice to draw the clansmen up in their ranks in the same order in which it was intended that they should fight; on arrival at the field of battle they would continue their march until the head of the column reached the extreme right of the position selected by the leaders, when the whole army would perform a simple left turn and confront the enemy. With a sufficiently sluggish opponent the method worked well enough.

Splashing through the Carron river, and inclining a little to their left as they marched at their usual rapid speed, the Highlanders soon found themselves well to the south of the town of Falkirk, with the heights which they were to occupy on their left front. Hawley had been lunching that day with Lady Kilmarnock, whose husband commanded a regiment of horse in the Prince's army—and was afterwards to lose his head for it. The General enjoyed his lunch, and, whether intentionally or not, the lady upon whom he had quartered himself seems to have exercised all her charm to keep him by her side. Suddenly news was brought of the Prince's movement and that the royal army was already broken up from its camp.

Rushing from the house, Hawley sprang upon his horse and rode, bareheaded, to the field. Arrived there, he hurriedly formed the dragoons into his first line and sent them forward to seize the heights before the Highlanders could reach them. The latter, having continued their march until the leading files of the Keppoch Macdonalds reached the edge of a small morass marking the extreme right of the position, now faced left and advanced rapidly up the slope towards the heights, with the same object in view. A clash was inevitable.

One word as to numbers. The Prince had left a thousand men in the trenches before Stirling and was probably about eight thousand strong. Since his junction with Lord Lewis Gordon and Lord John Drummond further reinforcements had arrived from the north. "They looked mighty well, and were very hearty," says Maxwell of Kirkconnel, who saw them. "The Macdonalds, Camerons, and Stuarts were almost double the number that had been in England; Lord Ogilvie had got a second battalion much stronger than the first. . . . In fine, all were at hand in high spirits, and expressed the greatest ardour upon the prospect of a battle."

The Hanoverians were equally confident, and they knew that they had the advantage in numbers. Hawley himself admitted afterwards that he was stronger than his opponent by two thousand men.

But the weather had changed. Captain Daniel, riding with the Jacobite horse, had noted at 2 P.M. that "the day, from being an exceeding fine one, became on a sudden obscure." He must have been looking over his shoulder, for it was behind the Highland army that the black storm-clouds began to rise. And now, as they reached the crest of the hill and saw before them for the first time the long line of scarlet-clad English dragoons already topping the rise on the other side and almost within musket shot, the rain swept savagely across their backs, and full into the faces of their opponents. In this respect Lord George Murray's plan of marching in a half-circle had succeeded better than he knew.

The opposing lines continued to advance. There were some preliminary manœuvres. Lord Elcho's horse had been unable to get to the right of the Macdonalds, as ordered, to protect their flank, because of the small morass already mentioned. The English dragoons made a feint in that direction in the hope of drawing the Macdonalds' fire. It failed. Lord George Murray was marching on foot in front of the Highland line. He carried a musket, and his orders were explicit that not a shot must be fired until he discharged his own piece. It would appear that the dragoons were on slightly higher ground than the Highlanders. Daniel was with the Jacobite light horse—numbering only four hundred and very conscious of their inferiority—now posted between the first and second lines—*i.e.*, with the Macdonalds in front of them and the Lowland brigades behind. Over the heads of the clansmen he could see the advancing dragoons, and "I must acknowledge that when I saw this moving cloud of horse, regularly disciplined, in full trot upon us down the summit, I doubted not but that they would have ridden over us without opposition." What professional soldier, indeed, could have doubted it!

They were so close now that Daniel could even hear them cursing in their English voices as the rain beat in their faces, blinding horses and men alike. Fifteen yards . . . they had lengthened their stride into a gallop . . . twelve yards . . . ten. Lord George Murray lifted his musket to his shoulder and fired at a dragoon in front of him, and immediately that long-delayed volley rolled out all along the line. The clansmen were probably the worst marksmen in any army in Europe, but the range was so short that they could not miss. Eighty is the lowest estimate of the number of horses that went down, kicking in the mud, at that first discharge. The advancing line broke into fragments within ten yards of its objective. Most of the dragoons, without more ado, turned their horses and rode for safety. A few, carried on by their own impetus, dashed in among the Highlanders, and for five minutes there was some brisk work, the horsemen slashing out right and left, the clansmen lying down and stabbing upwards with their dirks at the horses' bellies. Macdonald of Clanranald afterwards told Johnstone that

> whilst he was lying upon the ground, under a dead horse, which had fallen upon him, without the power of extricating himself, he saw a dismounted horseman struggling with a Highlander; fortunately for him, the Highlander, being the strongest, threw his antagonist and having killed him with his dirk came to his assistance, and drew him with difficulty from under the horse.

It was over in a few minutes, and the dragoons were gone. There were three regiments of them—Ligonier's and Hamilton's on the left, Cobham's on the right. The two former, having turned their horses, galloped off the field in confusion and were seen no more. Cobham's turned to the right and rode along between the two armies, losing heavily as they went, until they were able to encircle their own right wing and take refuge behind the infantry. It is necessary to explain how this could have happened. In the hurry of the advance up the hill the dragoons had found themselves opposite the Highland right and right centre, and it was against these that their charge had been directed. But the long line of royal infantry struggling up the hill behind them in the blinding rain had arrived not exactly opposite their opponents, but with their right wing overlapping the Highland left, and their left similarly overlapped by the Macdonalds. It is thus that Hamilton's and Ligonier's dragoons found the ground clear of infantry behind them when they turned to fly, whereas Cobham's on their right had to run the gauntlet between the opposing lines. Moreover, it was now seen that there was a "ravine" [1] between the

---

[1] Home. He was serving on foot with the Whig volunteers, and he is by far the best historian of the battle (I am using his map). Lumisden, Prince Charlie's private secretary, calls it an " unequality of the ground." Others ignore it.

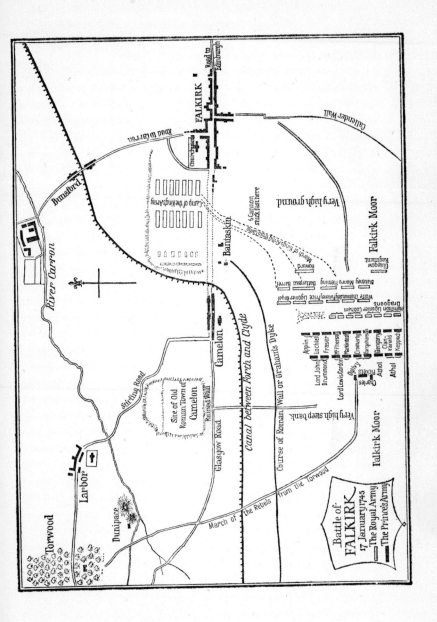

Battle of
FALKIRK
17 January 1745
The Royal Army
The Prince's Army

right of the Hanoverians and the left of the Highlanders which prevented the infantry on that side from closing.

The Macdonalds after their successful volley were ordered by Lord George Murray to halt and keep their ranks. Wiping the rain from their eyes and staring eagerly through the mist, they could at first see nothing in front of them; but presently the exposed left wing of the royal army came in sight on their left front, its flank entirely unprotected by cavalry. It included all the Whig volunteers, among them the Glasgow regiment, whom the Highlanders had no cause to love. This was more than the Macdonalds could stand. First in batches, then in whole regiments, they flung aside their muskets, and, seizing their broadswords, dashed across the hillside, yelling their war-cries. Lord George Murray was on foot among the clansmen; by great personal exertions he succeeded in holding back most of the Keppoch Macdonalds who were immediately behind him; but those of Clanranald and Glengarry on his left, with the Farquharsons and Mackintoshes beyond them, he could not control. Irresistible as ever, they broke in among the redcoats and Whig volunteers, driving them headlong from the field in the direction of Falkirk and doing considerable execution. Nothing could stop them. The very pipers had thrown away their pipes and joined in the charge, so that it was now impossible to sound the recall. Some of them followed their enemies into the streets of Falkirk; some clustered in knots at the foot of the hill; while others might be seen toiling slowly up the slope again to rejoin their commander. Of Lord George Murray's victorious right wing, only about half remained upon the field of battle.

On the left wing it had been a very different story. Lord John Drummond was in command. Here also the Highlanders nearest the centre charged and broke their opponents; but the majority were held up on the edge of the ravine, across which they endeavoured to maintain an unequal musketry duel with the regulars on the other side. They were quickly forced to retire—some even left the field. Cobham's dragoons, having re-formed, attacked their left flank. Accounts of this part of the battle are very confusing. In the failing light and the blinding rain it was difficult to see what was happening.

One thing alone is certain—that it was Prince Charles in person who by his intervention saved the situation. He had posted himself in the centre, in reserve. Coming up now with the Irish "pickets," who were under his immediate command, and other troops of the reserve, he passed the ravine on his left, and saw the unbroken regiments of the Hanoverian right, Barrel's, Price's, and Ligonier's foot, drawn up "in a hollow of the hills." The Prince halted and began to rally the Highlanders, who were drifting about all over the hillside with their broadswords in their hands. As soon as they saw his flag they ran to join him, and he was presently strong enough to advance. Cobham's dragoons, who were about to attempt another charge, immediately retired before him. The infantry followed suit, though still showing a bold front, and the whole force presently retreated in good order through the town of Falkirk.

So ended this scrambling, floundering affair of Falkirk, one of the most clumsily conducted battles in modern warfare. It will be noted that Lord George Murray, the wily strategist, made almost every possible tactical mistake. He marched on foot at the head of a clan—what a place for a general!—so that he was unable to control his line. Elcho, his friend, complains that nearly all the Jacobite leaders were allowed to do the same. He had assured the Prince that he knew the ground, yet he led the army to a position where there was a deep ravine between his left wing and the enemy's right. He must have known, if he had the slightest understanding of the fine fighting instrument under his command, that the Highlanders' weakest point was their musketry fire, the strongest their charge. Yet he got his left wing into a position where they could not charge, but could only shoot; and when his right wing, with a volley at ten yards' range, had shattered the cavalry, and had shaken the morale of the few infantry opposed to them, he tried to hold back their charge and make them stand firm. Against what? There is universal agreement, even among his friends who were present, that he ought to have unleashed them at once. He complained afterwards that Lord John Drummond was not present with the left wing and issued no orders. This was a mere *tu quoque* retort to one who was his principal critic. All the leaders, being on foot, were lost after the first clash (O'Sullivan was never seen at all!). The one exception was the Prince. He it was who, by prompt and vigorous action at the decisive moment, turned what looked like a draw into a win.

The astonishing confusion of the battle continued for hours afterwards. Macdonald of Tiendrish had an unfortunate adventure which illustrates this. Joining in that first wild charge, he had chased some of the Glasgow men through the streets of Falkirk; but, finding hardly any Highlanders there, he had returned to the scene of action to collect some more of them and complete the victory. As he did so he perceived, through the mist, a formed body of men coming slowly down the hill towards him. Assuming these to belong to his own victorious army, he ran towards them, calling out to them to mend their pace. Before he knew what had happened he found himself in the middle of Barrel's regiment, which, as related above, was making its orderly retreat. All round him were the black cockades of

Hanover. His own white one was so splashed with mud that for a moment he hoped he might not be recognized. But some one called out: "Here's a rebel!" When he offered to surrender General Huske, who was with them —Hawley's second-in-command and a bully like his chief —roared out: "Shoot the rebel down!" However, a Scottish officer came forward and courteously accepted his sword. So Tiendrish had the melancholy distinction of being the only Jacobite officer taken prisoner at Falkirk. He was executed a few months later at Carlisle.

Night had fallen when General Hawley, having set fire to his tents, began to retreat at his leisure down the road to Edinburgh. Some fifteen hundred of the Highlanders were in Falkirk, but the Prince and, apparently, all the other leaders were still out on the hillside, searching for their men or huddled under cover against the rain. When they saw the glare of the burning tents they supposed that some houses in Falkirk had been set alight. It is said that Lord Kilmarnock was the first to send news of the enemy's retreat, he having galloped towards his own house, where he found his fair lady none the worse for her encounter with the foe. It was eight o'clock or thereabouts before the Prince got the news. It was impossible to form the clansmen into any semblance of an army. "Not fifty could be brought together to continue the dispute," says Lumisden. As the leaders entered the town their men slipped away on every side in the darkness to seek shelter and warmth in the houses. Some of them had gone all the way back to their old quarters at Bannockburn! There were not even enough to guard the prisoners, many of whom had to be set free—including some of Hawley's executioners from Edinburgh.

Yet, as Maxwell of Kirkconnel says, "the victory was

complete." Our old friend Captain Daniel was among those sent to count the dead. He describes how they found "near seven hundred of the enemy slain" (this is probably an exaggeration) and about fifty of their own men. Among the former was Sir Robert Monro of Foulis, an enormously fat man, who had ridden into battle accompanied by his brother, a doctor (also slain). Sir Robert had been killed by a sword-cut across the mouth received, according to Daniel, at the very moment when he was violently cursing the hailstorm that blew in his face.

Hawley had lost his guns and all his tents, with much ammunition and baggage; nearly seven hundred of his men were prisoners. He could not understand it. "Our left is beat, and their left is beat," he wrote to Cumberland. Yet they had won. "My heart is broke." The "scandalous cowardice" of his men was horrible. (It may be added here that, on arrival in Edinburgh, he set about restoring the morale of his army in a manner peculiarly his own: he ordered thirty-one dragoons to be hanged "for deserting to the rebels" and "thirty-two of the foot to be shot for cowardice.")

The young Prince occupied Hawley's quarters in Falkirk. He was, not unnaturally, in a mood of considerable elation. The Highland charge had succeeded once again. The enemy was fled. And fate had given him an unexpected opportunity of displaying his own gifts as a leader. "The Prince," wrote Sheridan in his report of the battle to the Kings of France and Spain, had been "conjured for the love of his troops not to expose himself"; but "as soon as the left wing was thrown into some disorder, he flew to their relief with an ardour which was not to be restrained." He had shown that he possessed a soldier's eye; and witnesses have testified that it was his personal prestige and gallant bearing that rallied the clans so quickly at the critical moment of the day.

There was, however, some doubt as to the next step. Should they pursue Hawley into Edinburgh or resume the Stirling siege? Thanks to bad weather, bad discipline, and Lord George Murray's tactics, Hawley had got clean away. If they followed him now it was still pretty well certain that they could take Edinburgh, but not so certain as it would have been if they had entered the city at his heels. Many of the Prince's advisers "were for following the blow, and driving Mr Hawley out of Scotland"; while "some were for marching directly to London, without giving the enemy time to recover from their consternation." There was much to be said for that point of view. In three successive engagements against regular troops the Highland charge had swept all before it. Now was the time to press the advantage home. On the other hand, it seemed only logical to the military mind to pause first and bring to a rapid conclusion that siege of Stirling Castle which Hawley had vainly attempted to raise.

What turned the scale was the report of the French engineer, M. de Mirabel, or Mirabelle, who had been sent out by Louis XV as a siege expert with the heavy guns. If the Chevalier Johnstone can be believed this person was a mere clown. He was totally ignorant of military engineering, and, "his figure being as whimsical as his mind, the Highlanders, instead of M. Mirabel, called him always Mr Admirable." He was an invincible optimist, cheerfully undertaking to open trenches on the hills to the north of Stirling, though the soil was but fifteen inches deep above the solid rock, and the 'trench' must consist entirely of sandbags; and now, after Falkirk, solemnly promising the surrender of the castle within a few days. In the event his breastworks were easily knocked to pieces by Blakeney's guns, and the Lowlanders and Irishmen who manned them lost heavily. In the meantime, however, his reports were believed, and it was decided to make a rapid end of Stirling before attempting any further stroke. The Lowlanders were ordered back to their trenches. The Highlanders, who were useless for such work, were left at Falkirk. And the Prince returned to Bannockburn—and Clementina.

When the news of Falkirk reached London there were only two cheerful faces at the Court of St James—that of King George, who continued to say "Pho!" and that of General "Johnnie" Cope, which was observed to be wreathed in smiles. Johnstone says that Cope "had, according to the English custom, offered bets to the amount of ten thousand guineas in the different coffee houses in London that the first General sent to command an army against us in Scotland would be beaten, as he had been"; so that he had now "gained a considerable sum of money, and recovered his honour to a certain degree." But the general atmosphere was one of gloom. Not consternation, be it noted: nothing like the panic occasioned by the Prince's arrival at Derby. Somewhere up in the North there had been a set-back—unexpected and humiliating, no doubt, but only a set-back after all. The Government acted promptly. The Duke of Cumberland himself, with all the prestige of his family connexion and his military experience, was ordered to Scotland to clean up the mess. He left immediately, and arrived at Edinburgh on the 29th of January. There he put a stop to Hawley's executions—which were too much even for the "Butcher's" stomach—and took over the command of his army, reinforced by two regiments of foot and Lord Mark Ker's dragoons.

He made another and characteristic gesture. We have seen how Prince Charles, both from inclination and policy, was almost over-anxious to observe the courtesies of war. After Falkirk his first care had been to collect the bodies of Sir Robert Monro and the other Hanoverian officers who had fallen and bury them reverently. Finding himself unable to look after all his prisoners, he had set many of them free. Most of the English officers taken at Prestonpans were already in Edinburgh, living at their ease on parole. Cumberland now publicly absolved these officers of their oaths—and to their shame it must be stated that the great majority of them took him at his word and returned to their regiments. "The decay of virtue and honour in our Island since the [Hanoverian] Accession is very remarkable," comments Maxwell of Kirkconnel bitterly, "but hitherto a gentleman's word of honour had been looked upon as sacred."

The Jacobite army lay at Falkirk and Stirling. Things were not going well with them. The siege of Stirling Castle "went on but slowly," says Daniel, and "the spirit of the army began much to change"—a significant admission. The Lowlanders and Drummond's men who manned M. Mirabel's trenches felt that they were doing all the work and were, moreover, suffering unnecessary losses under the orders of a fool.[1] The cavalry were kept so busy scouting for the first signs of Cumberland's advance that they seldom slept in their beds. On the other hand, the Highlanders at Falkirk, having nothing to do, began to drift away towards their homes among the hills. An unfortunate accident on the very day after the victory of Falkirk accelerated this movement. One of the Macdonalds, either a Keppoch or a Clanranald, carelessly discharged his musket in the street, and the

---

[1] One critic thought that the Frenchman was perpetually drunk; but it may be only that he seemed so to a Scot. Lord George Murray agrees that he was "so volatile that he could not be depended upon."

THE DUKE OF CUMBERLAND
Sir Joshua Reynolds
National Portrait Gallery   182

bullet struck and killed Colonel Æneas Macdonald, Glengarry's second son. The effect upon the Macdonalds was extraordinary. To appease them the slayer was immediately hanged, though the thing was plainly an accident; but nothing could restore their spirits. Desertions from the ranks of Glengarry and Keppoch increased daily.

It was, in fact, the most insane kind of strategy to undertake a difficult siege with an army of which the most important part was incapable of siege operations. Once again it convicts Lord George Murray of an astonishing failure to understand the special character of the army he led—its limitations no less than its virtues. He was obsessed by those unlucky French siege guns. "Who could have imagined," exclaims Johnstone, "that the six pieces of heavy artillery sent by the Court of France to our assistance would have become our ruin?" Johnstone was one of the many officers who thought that by the failure to follow Hawley to Edinburgh a great chance had been thrown away.

What was needed was action—something for the Highlanders to do. So thought the Prince, and so will think most modern students of the Forty-five. The news that Cumberland was at Edinburgh and about to march out against him seemed good news to Prince Charles. He sent his secretary, Murray of Broughton, to interview Lord George Murray, and acquaint him with the Prince's intentions, "which were to go and attack the Duke of Cumberland when he advanced as far as Falkirk." It is unfortunate that neither of the two Murrays has left us an account of this meeting. Murray of Broughton's memoirs break off at Derby, and are not resumed until Culloden. Lord George makes no mention of any such message from the Prince. Maxwell of Kirkconnel, our only authority, is a cautious historian who hated Murray of Broughton but was well disposed towards Lord George. His account is as follows:

> Lord George seemed to approve of everything, drew up a new plan of battle, with some improvements upon the former, and sent it next day to the Prince for his approbation. The Prince was extremely pleased with the plan, and in the highest spirits to think he was to have to do with the Duke of Cumberland in person. But this joy was short....

That very night, in fact, he received to his amazement a communication, signed by Lord George Murray himself and the chiefs of the clans, urging the necessity of an immediate retreat to the north. They represented that "a vast number" of Highlanders had already deserted, and that "this evil is increasing hourly notwithstanding all the endeavours of the commanders." They spoke vaguely of the "inequality of our numbers to that of the enemy," and expressed the view that Stirling Castle could never be taken before the Duke was on top of them. They referred to the inclemency of the weather and promised the usual rally of "10,000 effective Highlanders" when they got to the North, ready "to follow your Highness wherever you think proper." It was a pity about the French siege artillery, but it would be better to throw it into the river Forth than risk the Prince's person and the flower of his army by remaining where they were.

I do not think that the receipt of this communication can have been quite such a shock to the Prince as some of the chroniclers have suggested. For instance, I do not myself believe that, after Derby, he ever had any real hope of winning back his throne. But the futility, not to say insincerity, of the arguments employed, and the spirit of defeatism which so obviously inspired them, were too much for his temper. Hay of Restalrig, who took the paper to him early in the morning, says that after reading it he sprang out of bed and struck his head violently against the wall, exclaiming: "Good God, have I lived to see this!"

So they were to run away again. Another victory was to be turned into a rearguard action. Under the pretence of preventing the Highlanders from deserting they were to remove still nearer to the Highlanders' homes. He understood his officers now. They had fought all the time like beaten men, thinking always of their line of retreat. He alone among them had the will to win.

Meantime he sent a dignified, unanswerable reply, pointing out the fatal moral effect of such a flight, asking what was to become of their Lowland friends if they deserted them, but indicating at the same time that he would not stand out against their united will. And when his officers retorted with a repetition of their former arguments he wrote this final and prophetic word:

> I know I have an army that I cannot command any further than the chief officers please, and therefore if you are resolved upon it I must yield—but I take God to witness that it is with the greatest reluctance, and that I wash my hands of the fatal consequences which I foresee but cannot help.

CHAPTER XI

CULLODEN

THE retreat to Inverness began on the 1st of February, 1746. The circumstances were such as might have shaken the discipline of the steadiest regular troops. The clansmen, says Elcho, were "struck with amazement" when they got the order, for "everybody expected a battle and it appeared very strange to run away from the very army that had been beat only a fortnight before." Strange, but no longer unusual : to run away after a victory was becoming the normal procedure. It is scarcely surprising, however, that the retreat soon came to resemble a flight. "There was hardly the appearance of an army." They crossed the river outside Stirling in small parties, leaving carts and cannon scattered along the road behind them. Scarcely had they cleared the town when there was a loud explosion in the rear, and the Prince, sending back to know what had happened, learned that the little church of St Ninian's, where some of the gunpowder was stored, had been set on fire by accident and blown sky-high. At Crieff he halted and reviewed his troops—only to find, to his disgust, that the number of the desertions had been grossly exaggerated. So that the last excuse for forcing this disastrous retreat upon him had disappeared !

The weather was terrible. At a formal council of war at Crieff (the first since Derby and the last that Charles ever called) it was decided to divide the army, the Prince leading the clans direct to Inverness by the Highland road, while Lord George Murray, with the

Lowland regiments, took the coast road through Montrose and Aberdeen. Daniel, who was with Murray's column, has left a vivid account of the sufferings of the troops. They were moderately comfortable at Montrose, "a fine loyal sea-port town"; and even at Aberdeen, though the local preachers inveighed against them all the time they were in the town.[1] But

> when we marched out of Aberdeen it blew, snowed, hailed and froze to such a degree that few pictures ever represented winter, with all its icicles about it, better than many of us did that day; for here men were covered with icicles hanging on their eyebrows and beards ; and an entire coldness seized all their limbs, a severe contrary wind driving snow and little cutting hail bitterly down upon our faces, in such a manner that it was impossible to see ten yards before us.

Daniel himself fell exhausted in the snow, and must have perished had he not brought a small flask of spirits in his riding-coat, half of which he poured down his own throat and half down that of his horse, and so came staggering into the town of Old Meldrum.

The Prince meantime had marched with his Highlanders to Castle Menzies, and thence to Blair, Dalnacardoch, Dalwhinnie, Ruthven (where he stormed the Hanoverian barracks), and Moy Castle, the home of the Lairds of Mackintosh. Here a characteristic adventure befell him, of a kind that most other young princes in history have sighed for in vain. It will be remembered that, whereas the Laird of Mackintosh was serving with the royal troops under Loudoun at Inverness, his lady

---

[1] They were "savage mountaineers," "ragged ruffians of the North," "thieves and murderers," followers of the "bloody house of Stuart," "starving banditti," who committed "shocking barbarities"; while the children in the streets were taught to cry out against "Charlie, prince of the robbers" (*The Lyon in Mourning*, vol. ii). As a matter of fact there has seldom been a better behaved army. For any parallel to these Whig libels we must turn to the literature of the rival propaganda departments in the Great War.

was of the contrary opinion and had raised her husband's clan in the Jacobite cause. She was still in residence at Moy Castle and gave the Prince a royal welcome when he arrived there on the 16th of February. The situation was not without humour, for Moy is only eight miles from Inverness, where Mackintosh was doing garrison duty on the other side. He and Loudoun seemed to have talked things over, with the result that the latter conceived the daring idea of a night march upon Moy, with the object of seizing the Prince's person.

But the Dowager Lady Mackintosh, the Laird's mother, was also in residence in Inverness. She heard of his plan and immediately despatched a messenger, young Lachlan Mackintosh, a boy of fifteen, to warn her daughter-in-law. The boy saw Loudoun's kidnapping party already on the march, but took a short cut across country and arrived panting at Moy Castle a little before them. As he reached the gates he raised a loud outcry, and, entering the kitchen, he seized hold of Alexander Stewart, who was sound asleep with his head on the table (for they had all dined well that night in honour of the royal visit), and shouted in his ear that he must go upstairs and wake the Prince. But the Prince was already looking over the banisters asking what was the matter. He came down quickly in his slippers and his nightcap, and there was a great to-do while the more valuable of his papers and other possessions were gathered together and he and his few followers were hustled out of the house before the enemy should arrive.

In the meantime, however, the blacksmith of Moy, a hero named Fraser, had been sent out with four companions to reconnoitre. They hid among the trees at either side of the road and waited there in the darkness. Presently they heard the tramp of marching men coming from the direction of Inverness. The column was a strong one, and Loudoun himself marched with it, for he was determined to be in at the capture of this royal stag. The blacksmith was fully equal to the situation. As the leading files reached his hiding-place he fired his piece into the midst of them, killing one of Loudoun's men and at the same time raising loud cries of "Advance, my lads, advance!" mentioning various of the clans by name, "We have the dogs now!" and so forth. A panic seized the Hanoverians. They turned and fled headlong down the road to Inverness, trampling underfoot the officers who attempted to check their flight. One of these Whig officers told Home, the historian, many years after, that though he had been on many stricken fields, he had never felt his life in such peril as when his own men trod him down in the mud on the road between Inverness and Moy. Prince Charles himself unfortunately missed this exhilarating encounter. From the point of view of his biographer the chief importance of the affair is that, paddling about in his nightcap and slippers, he managed to catch a fresh cold, and when he arrived at Inverness a few days later became definitely ill and was finally forced to take to his bed.

The affairs of the Jacobite army during the halt at Inverness, which lasted from the 18th of February until the battle of Culloden on the 16th of April, a period of about two months, were of comparatively little interest in the life of Prince Charles. During a large part of the time he was seriously ill with a cold and fever; from the 11th of March to the 20th he was unable to leave his room. He was then staying at Elgin. Before that date he had visited the Dowager Lady Mackintosh and thanked her personally for her timely warning; and as soon as he was well enough he returned to Inverness, and there kept open house, dining in public, dancing with his guests in the evening, going on shooting expeditions in the day-time, and generally exerting himself to win the favour of the local gentry. It was a last despairing effort, and I think he knew it.

But while the Prince was out of action there had been some lively skirmishes between his supporters and those of King George, which must be briefly described. They may be classified under three headings : first, the activities of Lord Loudoun and the Inverness garrison ; second, the Jacobite attempt to capture Fort Augustus and Fort William, the two Hanoverian outposts in the Highlands; third, Lord George Murray's campaign in his own country to the south.

Loudoun, on the approach of the Prince's Highlanders, had evacuated Inverness and retired across the Moray Firth to Black Isle, taking the garrison (and President Forbes) with him. And there he sat on the beach, glaring across the narrow waters at Inverness, while the King's ships held the sea in between. When the Jacobites marched round the head of the Firth to dislodge him he retired to the northern hills, and as soon as they had gone he appeared on the beach again. As he cut off all communication between the Prince and the North of Scotland, it was important to disperse his little force ; and at last, one foggy night, the Duke of Perth, with eighteen hundred men, managed to slip across the Firth in fishing-boats, unperceived by the English ships, and, falling suddenly upon Loudoun's camp, scattered his men so effectually that they never reassembled again.

The attempt against Fort Augustus and Fort William, conducted by Brigadier Stapleton, commanding the Irish and French auxiliaries, with Lord Lewis Drummond and some of the Camerons and Macdonalds of Keppoch, was not so successful. The Highlanders hated sieges, and it is more than doubtful whether these isolated forts with their tiny garrisons were worth the effort. Fort

Augustus was taken, but Fort William easily withstood
the fire of Stapleton's six-pounders, the heaviest siege
artillery he possessed.

Now, the countries of Atholl and Perth to the south of
Inverness were at this time almost denuded of fighting
men, since most of the Murrays were serving with Lord
George in the Prince's army; and the Hanoverians had
taken the opportunity to occupy these districts with
some of the Hessian troops newly arrived from Germany,
and with several regiments of Campbells, the Murrays'
hereditary foes. Accordingly, when Lord George Murray
received the Prince's order to clear out some of these
invaders he was undertaking a congenial task and set about
it briskly. With Macphersons and Mackintoshes and
men of his own clan he passed rapidly through the Atholl
country, mopping up the Campbell garrisons as he went.
At one place, Bun-Rannoch, he found a wake in progress,
and succeeded in capturing most of the mourners as well
as the corpse.

His triumphant progress was interrupted by the
approach of Sir Andrew Agnew, a blustering, choleric
officer, commanding the Hanoverian garrison at Blair.
Murray, who knew the sort of man he had to deal with,
hid his tiny force behind a dike, with their colours promi-
nently displayed, and ordered all his pipers to strike up
together as soon as Agnew's column came in sight. The
sound must have been terrifying, for the Hanoverians at
once retreated to Blair Castle. Murray followed and
laid siege to the place. Being without artillery, his only
hope was to bluff them into surrender. He dared not
send an officer to negotiate, for he knew that Agnew
would have ignored the white flag and hanged the 'rebel'
out of hand. He therefore bribed a good-looking maid-
servant from the inn at Blair to act as intermediary.
The girl, whose name was Molly, boldly delivered her

message, which was received with shouts of laughter by
the young English officers collected round the castle gate.
One of them, however, "being of a timid temper, with a
constitution impaired by drink," was foolish enough to
carry the ultimatum to Sir Andrew Agnew himself, and
we get an amusing picture of the rubicund knight emerging furiously from his chamber, bawling out threats
against the rebel messenger, until poor Molly was glad
to pick up her skirts and bolt for safety, to the great
entertainment of the onlookers on both sides. Lord
George and his Highlanders were quite unable to make
any impression upon Blair Castle, and early in April they
retired towards Inverness to join the Prince.

But the Duke of Cumberland was approaching. With
a strongly reinforced army, he had advanced northward
from Edinburgh to Falkirk. There, finding that his
enemy refused battle, he had elected to follow the right
wing of the Jacobite army, under Lord George Murray,
which, as we have seen, had taken the coast road to
Inverness. Pursuing this route at a leisurely pace, the
Duke reached Aberdeen on the 27th of February, nearly
three weeks behind Murray. There, somewhat to the
general surprise, he remained for five or six weeks more,
receiving further reinforcements by sea from Leith, inspecting his men and generally strengthening his re-
sources. He must have had a well-founded instinct that
time was on his side.

There were two roads from Aberdeen to the river Spey,
which lay across the path to Inverness: one through Old
Meldrum and Cullen, the other through Inverurie and
Strathbogie. The Duke sent his advance guards forward
along both these roads, pushing Lord John Drummond's
cavalry before them. He himself left Aberdeen on the
8th of April with the main body. Everywhere the route

of the royal troops was marked by the flames of burning houses, the property of Jacobite gentry, and of the Episcopalian churches. Extraordinary stories are told of Cumberland's own behaviour and his brutal treatment of his hosts, whether Whig or Jacobite, so that many of the houses he had stayed in with his staff wore the appearance of having been sacked by a foreign invader. Marching from Cullen to Fochabers, they found the sea on their right hand. And "a pleasant prospect" it was, writes one of them, for the English warships could now be observed, sailing parallel with the line of march, some of them standing in close to the shore and firing their guns at a party of "rebel hussars" on the other side of the river Spey. Presently Lord John Drummond's main body came in sight "with their white flags displayed" and "making a formidable appearance" as they fell back towards Inverness. On the 12th of April Cumberland crossed the Spey. Somewhere beyond the hills ahead lay the plain of Culloden. He had made all his plans and was ready for the event. With a sort of ponderous efficiency, slowly as fate, he drew near to what was to be his only victorious battlefield.

At Inverness the morale of the Highland army showed signs of cracking at last. The clansmen, it is clear, were confident as ever of their ability to beat any enemy off the field (they were still winning every skirmish; Major Glascoe had just surprised and captured the whole Campbell garrison at Keith). But they had learned by bitter experience that their leaders were equally able to turn each success into a defeat. And now, for the first time, they found their pay in arrears. For more than a month before Culloden they were given a weekly allowance of oatmeal instead of money. There was great discontent at this. Elcho says that they "very often mutinied"; it is easier to believe him when he adds that a good many of them "threw down their arms and went home," for their homes were now close at hand.

With regard to the attitude of the officers, Elcho, as we have seen, was a prejudiced witness, but his grumblings at least give some idea of what was being said among his own and Lord George Murray's friends. The "people of fashion" were complaining once more that the Prince "did not seem to have the least sense of what they had done for him" (he realized, at any rate, that they had lost him his chance of a throne!), that he never consulted any-one but "his favourites, Sir Thomas Sheridan, Messrs O'Sullivan, Murray, and Hay" (Murray, the secretary, as a matter of fact fell ill about this time and never saw the Prince again), and always preferred the Irish to the Scotch. It does seem to be generally agreed that Hay of Restalrig, who had taken Murray of Broughton's place, managed the commissariat very badly, thus adding to the discontent. And it is certain that the Prince called no more councils —nor is it easy to blame him for that.

What he had apparently hoped to accomplish was a forced march against Aberdeen before Cumberland was ready to make his northern advance. But when he rose from his sick-bed he found his troops widely scattered— the Duke of Perth pursuing Loudoun in the north, Stapleton with the Irish pickets at Fort William, and Lord George Murray in the south. Then came this miserable shortage of money and the consequent mur-murings. In the circumstances it is hardly surprising that the tortoise beat the hare, and that when the Duke crossed the Spey on the 12th of April the Prince was still struggling with his difficulties at Inverness. Perth, Stapleton, and Lord George Murray had rejoined; but Lord Cromarty was still in the north with many of the best Highlanders—Macgregors, Mackinnons, and Mac-donalds; Cluny Macpherson was at Badenoch, and about half of the Frasers were still on their way to join the Prince. So that more than two thousand loyal clansmen were absent when the crisis came. Charles's total available strength was between five and six thousand men. Cumberland's was near nine thousand. He had reached Nairn on the 14th of April, and lay there on the 15th celebrating his birthday, which happened to fall on that date. That same morning the Jacobite army was drawn up in line on Culloden Moor.

Such being the situation of the two armies, any reader who has followed my narrative thus far will scarcely be surprised to hear that at this juncture Lord George Murray came forward with an ingenious plan for attacking the royal army at a disadvantage, thus offsetting their numerical superiority. Briefly, his proposal was to make an immediate night march upon Nairn, followed by the Highland charge at the first peep of dawn, when the English soldiers might be expected to be still sleeping off the effects of drinking the Duke's health the night before. From Murray's own account it seems doubtful whether the proposal came first from him, but, at any rate, he adopted it with enthusiasm. Anything, he thought, was better than waiting to be attacked on the open moor at Culloden, where he "did not like the ground"; thought it "certainly not proper for Highlanders." The Prince also was "keen for the attack"; it would give the men something to do and take their minds off the oatmeal.

So the column set off at 8 o'clock at night, Murray, as usual, in the van, Drummond in the centre, and the Prince, with the Duke of Perth, in the rear. Some of the Mackintoshes went ahead as guides. There is no more difficult operation in the whole range of the military art than a night march. The distance to be covered was about twelve miles; but before the head of the column had reached Culraick, six miles from Inverness, "near a hundred messages"—if Lord George Murray can be believed—had come from the rear, urging that the pace must be slower or all contact would be lost. About 1 o'clock in the morning Lord John Drummond rode up to the front, and he was followed soon afterwards by the Duke of Perth, both of them declaring that the rear could never get up in time for the attack unless a short halt were made. While the officers stood consulting by the side of the road O'Sullivan joined them and urged them to proceed; he said he had just come from the Prince, who was eager for the attack.

But Lord George Murray was beginning to lose heart. At their present rate of progress, he argued, it must be sunrise before they could reach Nairn. Finally he gave the order to retreat. The camp-fires of Cumberland's army were then already in sight. Some rumour of the decision must have reached the Prince, for he sent forward Hay of Restalrig to ascertain what was being done. Hay met the vanguard already faced about for retirement; he expostulated vigorously, but, as Murray says, "nobody minded him." "Where the devil are the men going?" asked the Prince, as the backward movement became apparent even where he was in the rear. When Hay came back and reported, he exclaimed that Lord George Murray had betrayed him—a statement he was to repeat frequently in later years. Then he seems to have had a word with Murray himself, and to have agreed that anyhow it was too late now: their chance had gone. Turning to those about him, " There is no help for it, my lads," he said, "march back to Culloden House"— his headquarters. Afterwards it turned out that Cumberland was quite unaware of the approach of his enemies, so that, according to a letter from Prince Charles to his father, the attack might have succeeded after all.

In the dim morning light the Highland army appeared

once more on Culloden Moor. The men were staggering with fatigue. There were no rations for them, not even an issue of oatmeal. Some, the majority, threw themselves down to sleep where they stood. Others went into Inverness and the villages round about to seek for food.

It is significant of the general demoralization in the Prince's command that his intelligence service, on the eve of Culloden, seems to have been less efficient than at any period in the campaign. It never apparently occurred to any of the leaders that it might be Cumberland's intention to continue his march against them as soon as the sun was up. If we may believe one who was present on the occasion[1] it was little better than an accident that they were not surprised. He says that when the retreat from Nairn began he and some others of Lord Elcho's life guards, who were in the rear, finding themselves ready to drop from their saddles with fatigue, determined to ride no farther, but dismounted and went into a wayside barn to sleep, having tied their horses' bridles to their ankles. They had slept only an hour or two when a woman came in to warn them that the Duke's cavalry were in sight. Hastily mounting again, they galloped into Culloden with the news. But another party of horse had been before them, and the Prince was already out on the moor assembling his men. It was a scene of wild animation and confusion. Pipes sounded shrilly, drums were beaten; Lord George Murray, Lord John Drummond, the Duke of Perth, and other leaders rode in, shouting their orders; clansmen, wakened from their slumbers, drifted across the plain in small parties, most of them more than half-asleep. Slowly they fell into line across the moor, their right resting upon the boundary wall of some enclosed property, their left near the sea.

[1] Sir Robert Strange, in his *Memoirs* (London, 1855), vol. i, p. 59.

To the modern visitor this fateful strip of moorland, scene of the final battle of the Forty-five, seems quite extraordinarily narrow. The distance between its northern boundary on the one hand and the graves by the road on the south which now cover the bones of the Highland dead appears hardly wide enough to have contained the opposing lines. Only a few yards to the east of the clansmen's cairn is the field where the English dead were buried. Trying to visualize the fight, you get the same feeling as at Salamis of being cramped for space. Yet Culloden Moor, like that more famous bay, has about it, in some mysterious way, the air of a place where great deeds have been done. A brooding silence hangs over it. At some time since the battle it was covered with trees, but these have now been cut down, only the thin tufts of yellow grass marking where they stood. The ground is still boggy, and the heather is growing again as it grew in the spring of 1746. On a sunny day the Black Isle may be plainly seen across the blue waters of the Firth, beyond where the Highland left wing approached the sea; but the morning of April 16, 1746, dawned damp and dismal, and if Prince Charlie saw the Isle at all and those dangerous English ships, he saw them through a mist.

The Jacobite army stood to arms, as their custom was, in the same order as on the previous day—that is to say, Atholl on the right, then Lochiel's Camerons, Stewarts of Appin, Frasers, Mackintoshes, Farquharsons, and Macleans, with the Macdonalds on the left. That was the first line. The second was composed of the Highland horse on the right, the Irish pickets in the centre, and Lord Lewis Gordon and Sir Alexander Bannerman on the left.[1] They numbered not much more than five thousand

---

[1] There is some doubt about the position of Glenbucket, but he was probably in the second line. A full statement of the opposing forces will be found in Blaikie's *Itinerary of Prince Charles Edward Stuart*.

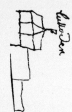

THE BATTLE OF CULLODEN

From a battle-plan made by Lord Elcho

men. Lord Cromarty, as already noted, was away in Sutherland; Cluny Macpherson, though expected every moment, had not yet arrived; near a thousand clansmen, exhausted by their efforts of the previous evening, are said to have lain asleep in the neighbourhood quite unconscious of the battle. The Macdonalds were on the left. They stood there in sullen silence.[1] In every previous engagement of the Forty-five they had fought on the other wing, and they held it to be their right, founded in history, to occupy the post of honour whenever they appeared on the battlefield for the royal house of Stuart. How the stupid mistake of placing them upon the left on this vital occasion came to be made is a controversial question and need not detain us here. It was done, and it could not be rectified.

Indeed, it would soon be too late to rectify anything. Already the Union flag and the red coats of the English soldiers could be seen at the other end of the corridor. The Highlanders stood waiting for them. It is difficult to know what was passing through the minds of the Jacobite leaders—not because we are without evidence, but because the witnesses disagree. Some declare that the Prince was against giving battle, but that Lord George Murray insisted upon fighting where they stood. Others assert the contrary. Murray, as we have seen, professes to have "disliked the ground": if Cumberland closed rapidly, or if he were foolish enough to attempt a cavalry attack, as at Falkirk, all might be well; but if he preferred to stand off and shoot it would be very difficult to press home the Highland charge across that open ground. There had been talk of crossing the river Nairn, to the right of the battlefield, and taking position among the hills, where the Duke could not follow. The advantage of this course was that they might have waited until the

---

[1] This is sometimes denied.

evening, collected all their men, perhaps received reinforcements, and then attempted another night attack ;
the disadvantage was that the Duke might have occupied
Inverness, and that in the meantime the Prince's men
would have been without food. Some say that this was
the Prince's plan, others that it was Lord George Murray's.
What we can unhesitatingly believe is Elcho's statement
that, in the general confusion on the morning of the
battle, it was never mentioned at all.

The two armies drew closer together. The Duke's full
strength had deployed upon the plain—two solid lines of
infantry, with his guns in all the intervals between the
regiments of the front line, his powerful cavalry on both
flanks. His total strength was nearly nine thousand men.
He moved forward slowly: a cautious, menacing, crab-
like advance, holding singularly little prospect of any
light-hearted cavalry attack, such as would have given
the Highland broadsword its chance.

But now the Prince was out in front of his army,
mounted on a handsome grey gelding. He wore a tartan
coat, with a buff-coloured vest. As he rode slowly down
the line, with his face to his men, the rain beat upon his
back and the wind blew his hair about his ears (for the
weather was against the Highlanders at Culloden, as it
had been with them at Falkirk). At the sight of him
the clansmen flung their bonnets in the air, raising
their battle-cries—and were answered, through the mist,
by the sound of English cheers. Gay and debonair as
ever (whatever he may have felt in his heart), he appeared
before his Highland army for the last time. Then he
turned his horse's head and rode to his position in the
centre of the second line.

Cumberland's guns began to play upon the opposing
ranks, and were answered by the Prince's scanty artillery,
posted on either flank. As the royal army drew nearer

the gunners loaded with grape and ploughed great paths
through the ranks of the Highlanders, who could do
nothing but stand and wait. Those, indeed, were their
orders—to remain where they were until the distance was
short enough for a charge. The cannonade continued
for an hour. They were losing heavily. Some threw
themselves on the ground—they should all have been
instructed to do so—but most remained on their feet,
enduring as best they might the hail of deadly missiles
that came to them through the mist. They were totally
unaccustomed to this cold-blooded kind of fighting. If
Cumberland had arranged every detail himself he could
not have asked for a situation better suited to his own
tactics, more fatal to those of his opponents.[1]

A round shot struck the ground within a few yards of
the Prince, throwing mud and stones in his face. A
groom, leading a sumpter horse, was killed at his elbow.
The Prince, seeing his followers falling all round him,
ordered the survivors to take shelter in a covered way.[2]
He himself rode off towards the right, freely exposing his
person and striving to animate his men in this terrible
ordeal. But, in spite of every effort, it seems clear that
a good many Highlanders had left the field before the
royal army came within musket range.

But the battle was not yet lost. Lord George Murray
commanded the right wing. He had endured not only
the cannonade from the front, but a galling fire from
some of the Campbells who had got among the enclosed
fields on his right. As the enemy came close enough to
use their small arms urgent messages reached him from

[1] The observant Johnstone remarks: " All kinds of firearms are directly at
variance with the natural disposition of the Highlanders, who are quick, ardent,
and impetuous in their attack. The sword is the weapon which suits them
best. When they are kept passive they lose their ardour."

[2] Colonel Belford, of the royal artillery, is said to have aimed these shots
deliberately, having observed the position of the Prince and his staff (Home,
The History of the Rebellion in the Year 1745).

the Prince.   At last, judging that his moment had arrived, he placed himself at the head of his Highlanders (no one had ever doubted his personal courage), and led a desperate charge against the royal regiments in his front.   Murrays, Gordons, and Stuarts, like hounds unleashed, sprang after him with a yell, and, covering the intermediate ground almost as quickly as it takes to tell it, burst in upon Barrel's and Monro's regiments and others of the Hanoverian left, breaking them in a moment and capturing two pieces of cannon.[1]

So far it was the story of Prestonpans and Falkirk over again.   But their numbers had been terribly reduced ; they became aware of a lack of support on their left ; they realized that they were almost alone, buried in the left flank of the royal army.   And at that moment the regiment of the second line, immediately behind Barrel's, appeared suddenly through the mist and attacked them resolutely.   It was Wolfe's regiment, commanded by the future hero of Quebec.   (At the beginning of the action they had been standing up to their ankles in water and had been moved out to their left front, so that they now took the Highlanders somewhat in flank.)   At the same time some of the guns, farther down the line to the right, were turned against them in a flanking fire.   They began to give ground—and with such troops that is the end. In a moment Lord George Murray's gallant right wing was scattered in flight, taking its leader with it.

The panic spread.   The Mackintoshes had broken out from the centre of the Jacobite line and, inclining a little to their right, had burst through the Hanoverian left centre, and found themselves opposite Sempill's and Blyth's regiments in the second line.   These had received them with a withering musketry fire, the front ranks

---

[1] For the names of the royal regiments I follow Home in preference to Elcho.

kneeling, the rear ranks firing over their heads. Some of the surviving Mackintoshes, continuing their charge, died upon the soldiers' bayonets, but the most part, turning back, joined in the general retreat of the right wing. The Farquharsons, next to them, seemed to have hung back. Surveying the scene, we note a disinclination to attack which becomes more and more marked as we move to the left. The Macdonalds, after exchanging volleys with the King's troops, threw away their muskets and drew their swords; but they made no general charge, and, seeing the Highlanders on their right repulsed, they fell back slowly to the second line. Yet not all of them. Macdonald of Keppoch, finding that his men would not follow him, rushed forward alone, sword in hand, a gallant figure. He was hit and fell, struggled to his feet, was hit again, and, within a few yards of the enemy, fell to rise no more.

The Duke was in no hurry. This method of fighting suited him admirably. The Highland right wing was now driven from the field; his horse were circling round the sullen ranks of the Macdonalds, ready to crumple them up as soon as the infantry should attack in front. A premature advance by Kingston's horse had been checked by a steady volley from the Irish pickets, now in line with the Macdonalds. But the latter were beaten men. When the whole of Cumberland's right wing moved forward against them, steadily as though on parade, they turned their backs and fled from the field in the direction of Inverness. Some of the right wing had crossed the Nairn and taken refuge among the hills; others fled immediately to their rear into Stratharick. The whole army was in headlong flight.

Just before the left gave way the Prince was seen desperately striving to rally some of the men from the centre. Tears were streaming down his face.

CHAPTER XII

THE ESCAPE

It has been said before, and is a wise saying, that it was after Culloden that Prince Charlie conquered Scotland. A born adventurer if ever there was one, it may very well be that he was not sorry, in his heart, to get away from the Lord George Murrays, the Elchos, and the other "men of fashion" and half-hearted advisers, and ride away into the heather to meet his fate alone. For in all the best adventures, as every schoolboy knows, there is an element of loneliness—of one man pitted against the world. The most popular literature produced by the Great War is what has been called its "escaping literature"—the journals of young officers who broke out from German or Turkish prisons and made their way across country, with many hardships and intolerably exciting games of hide-and-seek, to the nearest frontiers. And Bonnie Prince Charlie, the prince of escapers, must surely have felt some of this—may even have found his heart leap within him as he spurred his horse westward from Culloden field. If he had shed bitter tears as the full extent of the military disaster came upon him it was less for his own sake than for his brave Highlanders and his father's cause. And we who read the story of his life shall find that we get to understand him and know him better during these ensuing five months which he spent as a hunted fugitive than we ever did when he rode at the head of his army or dined in princely state at Holyrood.

As he rode from the battlefield he could hear the sound of the pursuit fading away to his right in the direction of

Inverness. Kingston's dragoons were chasing the flying Macdonalds to the outskirts of the town, and as they overtook them they hewed them down mercilessly, for neither then nor at any time did they give quarter—it was the Duke's orders. The Prince had with him about sixty of Fitzjames's horse and a number of officers, including Lord Elcho, Sheridan, O'Sullivan, Alexander Macleod, and others. His gallant grey had been hit in the shoulder as he was attempting to rally the right wing, and he was now mounted on a fresh horse. A man named Edward Burke ("a common chairman in Edinburgh") met them and offered to act as guide. Said the Prince: "If you be a true friend, pray endeavour to lead us safe off." "Which honour," comments Burke in an engaging journal he left behind him, "Ned was not a little fond of." With this Ned as guide, they galloped on steadily and crossed the river Nairn at the ford of Falie. Here Charles dismissed his cavalry escort, telling the men to seek their own safety, and rode on alone with the officers and the guide till he came to Gortleck House, where he met with Lord Lovat and other leading Jacobites and sat and drank three glasses of wine with them.

They discussed the situation, and, according to Elcho, Lovat advised him "not to quit the country, but stay and gather together again his scattered forces." Macleod, the aide-de-camp, at once sat down and wrote a letter to Cluny Macpherson, stating that there was to be a review of the clans at Fort Augustus on the following day and requesting him to be present. What the Prince thought about it we can only guess from his subsequent actions. Mounting his horse again at two in the morning, he rode on through the darkness, passed Fort Augustus without a pause, and arrived early on the day after the battle (the 17th of April) at Invergarry Castle. He rested until the afternoon, and then went on across country, with Burke,

O'Sullivan, and others, to Donald Cameron's house, a mere cottage, at Glenpean. Most of the Scottish officers had left him by now. He had eaten nothing, except some fresh salmon which Ned Burke had pulled out of the loch at Invergarry and cooked as best he could. Thinking that the tartan coat he wore at Culloden might betray him, he took it off, and Burke gave him his own coat instead.

Of all that gallant little army, scattered in flight from Culloden Moor, only one small remnant of any fighting value remained. Stapleton, with the Irish pickets and the other troops from overseas, had retired into Inverness, and there surrendered to Cumberland on terms. But the remains of the Highland right wing had crossed the river Nairn, as we have seen, and were all at Ruthven of Badenoch, on the way to Fort Augustus, some two or three thousand fugitives in all. There also were Lord George Murray, the Duke of Perth, Lord John Drummond (who had galloped from the field in company with our old friend Daniel), and the Chevalier Johnstone,[1] who was among those who thought that another stand might be made, and blamed the Prince for taking no action to that end. What actually happened it is difficult to say. Johnstone's account is quite unreliable, as Blaikie has shown. The men at Ruthven were entirely without supplies. Even Lord George Murray, though in resigning his commission he wrote a bitter letter to the Prince, agreed that "no hopes were left." Contradictory accounts of their situation reached the Prince. Finally (though on what day is not quite clear) he settled the matter by sending a message to Ruthven, thanking his friends for their devotion, but desiring that every man should take the steps which seemed best to him for his own safety. Looking back upon it now, it seems the wisest thing he could have done. According to Johnstone, there was dramatic leave-

---

[1] Johnstone and Daniel both escaped to the Continent.

taking when this last-formed body of Jacobites broke up; the officers shed tears, while the clansmen raised "wild howlings and lamentations." It marked the end of the Forty-five.

We left the Prince at Glenpean. The record of his adventures begins now definitely to take on the character of an escaper's log. The one fixed idea in his head was to get away from the mainland to the western isles, where first he had landed. It was not that he was thinking of the £30,000 (a vast sum in those days) which the Hanoverian Government had put on his head; again and again in the succeeding months he showed that he was prepared to trust the humblest fisherman with his life; but he longed to get the water between himself and his pursuers—at the moment that was his chief feeling. After only a few hours' rest, therefore, he and his party, discarding their horses, set out on foot across the hills and arrived next day (the 19th of April) in the braes of Morar, where they took refuge in "a small sheal house" and slept the sleep of exhausted men. On the 20th, at night, they walked to Borradale.

He was now in the country that he knew, for he had landed there when he came from France. Soon the loyal Macdonalds of the neighbourhood began to rally round him, as they had eight months before—or, if they did not come themselves, they sent their retainers. From the wife of Angus Macdonald of Borradale the Prince got a new suit of Highland clothes, "the better to disguise him." He remained four nights in this neighbourhood, and seems at first to have entertained the mad idea of sending for help to Sir Alexander Macdonald of Sleat or Macleod of Macleod, both of whom had steadily refused to have anything to do with his cause from the day of his landing. But as he walked one day in a wood by Borradale he fell in with a certain Donald Macleod, who had been sent to him

from Kinlochmoidart to act as his guide; and when he
stated his plans this wise old man—he was nearing seventy
—absolutely refused to carry any message to Sir Alexander
or Macleod. "What, does not your Excellency know that
these men have played the rogue to you altogether, and
will you trust them for a' that? Na, you mauna do 't."
The Prince looked at Donald and liked him—he was to like
this humble follower better still during the next few
weeks. He decided to place himself in his hands. "I
hear, Donald," he said (making no further reference to his
previous plans), "that you are a good pilot, that you know
all this coast well, and therefore I hope you can carry me
safely through the islands, where I may look for more
safety than I can do here."

Donald was his slave from that moment. He hurried
off at once to find a boat; and on the night of the 26th of
April the Prince and all his party—consisting of O'Sullivan, O'Neil (another Irish officer), Allan Macdonald (a
priest), Donald Macleod, Ned Burke, and seven boatmen
—went on board their little craft and pushed off from the
beach of Borradale—the very same beach, by a strange,
ironic stroke of fate, upon which he had landed in the previous July to begin his adventure. But the Prince cared
nothing for these things. He was beginning to enjoy himself. It was a dirty night, with promise of worse weather
to come, and his friends had advised him not to start; but
he had insisted. Now, from his place in the stern, where
he sat huddled in his new tartan cloak, he struck up a
Highland song to cheer his companions.

But the wind blew harder every moment, and presently
even Charles was fain to confess that he "had rather face
cannons and muskets than be in such a storm as this." He
even suggested that they might try running ashore on the
rocky coast by the side of the loch; but Donald abruptly
dismissed this proposal, and after that "all was hush and

silence " in the boat. They had no compass nor lantern
with them—nothing to guide them past the islands of
Rum and Eigg; but Donald's seamanship, coupled with
some of the luck that follows princes, brought them
through, and at the break of day they found themselves,
rather to their pilot's surprise, within easy reach of the
coast of the Long Isle, approaching Benbecula. They
landed, wet to the skin, and went to an empty fisherman's
hut, where they lit a fire and dried themselves. When
evening came they spread an old sail on the bare ground,
and the Prince laid down upon it, both this and the following night, and "was very well pleased with it and slept
soundly." Their objective was Stornoway, in the island
of Lewis—so they had settled it; on the next night (the
29th), therefore, they launched their boat again, and by
morning they had got as far as Scalpa, off the coast of
Harris, where they went ashore and took refuge at the
house of one Donald Campbell, a friend of Donald
Macleod's.

Their new host, in spite of his name, entertained them
most kindly, and they stayed with him four days. The
Prince would be up early in the mornings, roaming about
the farm and sometimes finding hens' eggs, which he
would beg of Mrs Campbell for his breakfast. His spirits
were rising all the time; yet Donald Macleod says that,
though he "would never own that he was in bad health,"
he was suffering from dysentery during the whole of this
period. If so the eggs were about the best thing he
could eat. He never slept more than three or four hours,
and on waking would call for a drink of water—another
good habit. Later he fell into the local custom of beginning the day with a dram, and before the end of his
wanderings would consume a bottle of brandy in the
twenty-four hours without turning a hair. A modern
Englishman of sedentary habits may find this shocking—

though a Scottish gillie might be less impressed—but Prince Charles was of the eighteenth century and was, moreover, leading an exceptionally hard outdoor life. Even in such circumstances a bottle of brandy a day, drunk with clear spring water, was no doubt a generous allowance; but it was not enough to impair his efficiency.

The Prince also carried in his pocket "a little bottle" from which he used to take a few drops at regular intervals —no doubt some kind of medicine; but not apparently for dysentery, for when Ned Burke became "unco ill of a colick" the Prince said: "Let him alane, I hope to cure him of that"—and so he did, with these same drops.

At Scalpa he heard from his enemies for the first time for a fortnight or so. The Rev. Aulay Macaulay (an ancestor of the historian), who was minister of Harris, and a fanatical Whig like his descendant, attempted to raise a party to come over to Scalpa and arrest the Prince. But Donald Campbell heard of it and headed them off. As a matter of fact, if the Prince had stayed at Borradale he could probably have got clean away to France; for while he was at Scalpa two French ships arrived, drove off the English sloops of war, and embarked a number of Jacobite officers who had remained on the mainland and were thus enabled to escape before their Prince.

But the Prince went on to Stornoway according to plan, landing in Harris and walking overland. It rained all the way, and when he came to Arnish, outside Stornoway, and entered the house of Mrs Mackenzie of Kildun, he and his companions were once more soaked to the skin. In fact, the three gentlemen, Charles, O'Sullivan, and O'Neil, had just six shirts between them, and were continually occupied with the problem of how to get something dry next their skins. Donald Macleod went ahead to Stornoway (he was trying to charter a ship to take them over to the Orkneys, but it appears he had got drunk and muddled the deal). Now, to his amazement, as he approached the town he found a great crowd of the inhabitants assembled in the roadway to warn him off. Mr Macaulay of Harris had written to them, and they were determined to have nothing to do with this dangerous affair. Not all Donald's threats and entreaties would move them. They would not betray the Prince, but neither would they help him. It was an awkward setback.

But the Prince, when he heard the news, refused to be downhearted. Burke was for flying to the hills. "How long is it since you turned cowardly?" exclaimed Charles. For his own part, he added, he would never be taken alive. Mrs Mackenzie had killed a cow in their honour; they made a hearty meal and lay down to sleep, while their clothes dried by the fire. In the morning Charles announced his intention of returning to Scalpa, so, taking the head of the cow and some other provisions with them, they put to sea again. But when they had got about twelve miles from land they sighted two warships and were obliged to run in to the uninhabited island of Iubhard. There were a few fishermen on the island, but these, having observed the King's ships in the offing, mistook the Prince's boat for the press-gang and decamped hurriedly, leaving a large quantity of dry fish lying on the beach.

Here was a great windfall, exclaimed the Prince as he sprang ashore. Some one protested that it was not their property, but Charles brushed these objections aside and, seizing an armful of fish, hurried up the beach to "a low pitiful hut," which was to be their home for the next two days. He was at the top of his form. While the others slept he and Ned Burke, who was the official cook, set to work to prepare a dish of fish. The Prince called for butter. Ned remembered that there was some in the boat, but it had got mixed with crumbled pieces of bread, and he was ashamed to offer it. "You are a child, Ned," said Charles; "the butter will do exceedingly well." He proceeded to boil the fish with it, and the three gentlemen presently made "a very hearty meal." But it is amusing to note that when Donald Macleod looked at the butter he, like the "common chairman," Ned, was revolted, and declared that "the deil a drap he would take."

The Prince also superintended the making of bread, according to his own recipe—the brains from the cow's head mixed with meal. It was "very good bread indeed." They found an old earthenware jar, and made warm brandy punch. The Prince gave the toast of "the black eyes"—though whether he was thinking of Clementina or of brunettes in general is uncertain. Many years afterwards Donald Macleod was asked about the ceremonial side of these meals. He protested indignantly that even on the desert island they always "kept twa tables, one for the Prince and the shentlemen and the other for the boatmen" (which would include himself and Burke). They sat on the bare ground, with big stones for their tables.

On the 10th of May they sailed to Scalpa, but found that their benefactor, Donald Campbell, had been compelled to go into hiding on their account, and therefore proceeded on their voyage. They sailed south for Benbecula, but were repeatedly headed off by the King's ships, one of which appeared suddenly round a headland almost within musket-shot. They escaped by rowing into shallow water. After a miserable night at sea, eating dramach (meal mixed with salt water), which only the Prince seemed to enjoy, they landed at Loch Uskavagh, in Benbecula, and stayed there three nights in a grass-keeper's "bothy," which was so low that the door had to be cut away to enable the Prince to enter, "he being tall." While they sat there eating a hurried meal of collops a "poor ragged boy" joined their party. Presently he thrust his hand into the dish uninvited. Ned Burke gave him a backhanded blow, but the Prince intervened and insisted upon his being allowed food and some rags of clothing. This boy, according to Burke, afterwards went and gave information to a party of Campbells who were out after the Prince. Fortunately they refused to believe him.

The presence of the King's ships made the sea unsafe, so the next move was an overland march to Coradale, in South Uist. Here the Prince and his party remained for twenty-two days in something like comfort. The menu improved immediately, for South Uist was reckoned the best place in all Scotland for grouse, partridge, and other wild fowl, not to mention deer. Charles was often out with his gun, "papping down perhaps dozens in a day," writes Burke admiringly—indeed, "scarce ever making a miss." He could imitate the call of the plover so cunningly that the birds flew towards him. Apparently he never went after deer, but "one day seeing a deer run straight towards him, and firing off-hand, he killed it"—quite a remarkable effort if, as one presumes, he had loaded only with duck-shot!

Macdonald of Boisdale came to see him, and three or four Scottish officers from Clanranald's regiment joined his party. He had sent off Donald Macleod to the mainland to get a fresh supply of money from Murray of Broughton or Lochiel, and he now waited anxiously for news. But his enemies were closing in on him on every side. The sea was full of English ships. Captain Ferguson, one of the naval officers, landed at Barra with a party of redcoats ; the Macleods of Skye were looking for him at Benbecula ; and the Campbells were on Uist.

It was clearly time to move. They sailed (on the 6th of June) to Ouia, where Donald Macleod (who had returned empty-handed from his mission to the mainland) and O'Sullivan remained, while the Prince and O'Neil walked on to Rossinish. They could do no good there, so Donald and O'Sullivan came in the boat and brought them off under cover of darkness. But a violent storm sprang up and drove the boat into Acarseid Fhalaich, where they "lay that night in the clift of a rock," the Prince sleeping peacefully with his bonnet pulled over his eyes. The hounds were within two miles of them. They went south to Boisdale and skulked up and down, sleeping in the open fields at night with the boat sails spread over them. It was obvious that the party must break up. They had been joined by Neil MacEachain, who was closely acquainted with the family of Miss Flora Macdonald of Milton on the other (or western) side of South Uist. The Prince decided to go with this man, taking only O'Neil with him. To the rest he bade farewell, paying off the boatmen and handing the faithful Donald a draft for sixty pistoles upon his secretary, Hay of Restalrig. It was never paid.

A fortnight later Donald Macleod was arrested and sent on board one of the warships. He was led into the cabin and cross-examined by General Campbell, who asked the usual leading questions. "Yes," said Donald, "I was along with that young gentleman, and I winna deny it." Campbell asked, "Do you know what money was upon the man's head? No less a sum than thirty thousand pounds sterling" (you can hear the Scottish accent), "which would have made you and all your children after you happy for ever." Donald's answer is historic. "Tho' I could have gotten all England and Scotland for my pains I would not allowed a hair of his body to be touched if I could help it." Even the Campbell understood that.

"I will not say that you are in the wrong," was his comment.

The Prince and his two companions walked across country towards Milton. O'Neil, who was scouting ahead, observed a lonely hut, and, approaching it cautiously, had the extraordinarily good fortune to find there Miss Flora Macdonald, the lady who was to save the Prince's life. Her grave, steadfast beauty has been preserved for us in a well-known painting. If MacEachain's hints can be taken seriously the impulsive young Irish adventurer, O'Neil, fell in love with her forthwith.[1] She listened calmly while he poured out the story of their misfortunes and their urgent need. Without mentioning Charles by name, he said that he had brought a friend to see her. She, with the first show of emotion, asked if it were the Prince. O'Neil said it was, and, giving her no time to reflect, rushed out of the hut and called Charles in. There was an earnest consultation—the Prince charming as ever, with that little touch of natural dignity; the lady deeply stirred.

It happened that Flora's stepfather was a captain in one of the "independent companies," as they were called, which had been raised by the Government for the express purpose of hunting down this young prince who now stood before her, so smilingly at his ease, his face tanned by the sun and rain. O'Neil wanted her to obtain an official pass which would enable the Prince, disguised as a servant, to pass over with her to the island of Skye, to the house of Lady Alexander Macdonald, and afterwards to the mainland. She demurred to this, though "with the greatest respect and loyalty," fearing that it might injure her relatives. But O'Neil, according to his own account, represented "the honour and immortality that would redound to her by such a glorious action."

---

[1] It is clear, however, that they were already acquainted.

For once the Irishman did not overdo the blarney. She was a brave, loyal girl, and presently she acquiesced and so won her place in history.

Having agreed to undertake this dangerous adventure, she acted with characteristic promptitude. That very night she set out, with MacEachain, for Clanranald's house at Nunton. At one of the fords they were arrested by a party of militia, out hunting for the Prince, and were kept in custody till the following morning, when her stepfather arrived. He set her at liberty, and, after hearing her story, at once made out passes for herself, MacEachain, and a female servant (the Prince), who was to pass under the name of Betty Burke. From Lady Clanranald she obtained a flowered linen gown, a white apron, and other garments, and hastened to join the Prince at a cottage where he had taken refuge from the militia, who were now prowling the country on every side.

He was in the act of superintending the roasting of his dinner, which consisted of the heart, liver, and kidneys of a bullock, impaled upon a wooden spit. Lady Clanranald and Mrs John Macdonald of Kirkibost were with Flora. O'Neil, who had guided them to the hut, hastened to introduce the ladies to the Prince. Charles made "his young preserver" sit on his right hand, with Lady Clanranald on his left, and "they all dined very heartily." His attitude towards Flora was clearly defined from the outset. "When she came into the room he always rose from his seat and paid her the same respects as if she had been a queen."[1] O'Neil's feelings towards her have already been indicated. He now begged hard to be included in the party for Skye, "but Miss could by no means be prevailed upon to agree to that proposal."

[1] Note by Bishop Forbes, editor of *A Lyon in Mourning*. On a later occasion, in the public room of an inn, when a quick change of clothes was required of him to avert capture, he refused to throw off his things in her presence.

FLORA MACDONALD
Allan Ramsay
Bodleian Library, Oxford 216

So the lovesick Irishman was left behind—to be captured soon afterwards, but released on parole in the following year.

The little boat set out for Skye at 8 o'clock on the evening of the 28th of June. Soon the sea became rough, and the Prince, as his custom was, began to sing to cheer his companions. Asked by Bishop Forbes, many years after, what songs he had sung, Flora said that they were *The King Shall Enjoy his Own Again*, and *The Twenty-ninth of May*. Presently she fell asleep, and Charles, leaning over her, guarded her carefully, lest any of the men, moving about the boat in the darkness, should tread upon her. They had only one half-bottle of wine with them, but the Prince would not let anyone touch it, keeping it, as Flora herself has told us, "altogether for Miss Macdonald's use, lest she should faint with the cold." They had no compass and knew not where they were; but in the morning made the point of Vaternish, at the north-west corner of Skye, and, avoiding a party of men who fired at them from the beach, rowed on to Kilbride, in Troternish, near Macdonald of Kingsburgh's house. Here Flora was handed from the boat, and hastened up to the house to arrange for their reception.

Charles was all this time in his woman's dress, and there were some amusing scenes when Kingsburgh came down and brought him up to the house. Kingsburgh's wife, who had not been let into the secret, was seriously alarmed, "for," said she, "I saw such an odd muckle trallup of a carlin making lang, wide steps through the hall, that I could not like her appearance at all." Kingsburgh told her who it was, and begged her to hasten supper, pointing out that there were eggs, butter, and cheese in the house. "Eggs and butter and cheese!" says Mrs Macdonald. "What a supper is that for a prince!" "Oh, good wife," said he, "little do you know how this prince has been living for some time past; these, I can assure you, will be a feast to him." And, indeed, Charles played a good knife and fork, as his habit was, and drank a bumper afterwards to his host and hostess. When supper was finished, bringing out "a cracked and broken pipe, wrapped about with thread," he asked Kingsburgh for a fill of tobacco.

They all slept well that night. In the morning Mrs Macdonald begged Flora to get her a lock of the Prince's hair. The latter modestly refused, but her hostess, taking her by the hand, knocked at Charles's door and explained the object of her mission. "Pray desire Miss Macdonald to come in," said he. "What should make her afraid to come where I am?" She sat timidly by the bedside, and he, "laying his arms about her waist, and his head upon her lap, desired her to cut out the lock with her own hands." She did so, and gave one half to Mrs Macdonald, keeping the other herself.

Next day they rode to Portree, where Kingsburgh had a boat waiting. As usual, it poured with rain, and they stayed some hours in an inn to dry themselves. The party was now to break up again, so that the time had come to say good-bye to the girl who had undoubtedly saved his life. Charles was once more dressed as a man, in Highland clothes borrowed from Kingsburgh. He turned to Flora. It was the end of that almost perfect relationship between a prince and a maid which has delighted the whole world ever since. He said:

"I believe, madam, I owe you a crown of borrowed money." She told him it was only half a crown, which accordingly he paid her with thanks. He then saluted her, and expressed himself in these or the like words, "For all that has happened I hope, madam, we shall meet in Saint James's yet." [1]

With that he was gone, and Flora was left alone with her

[1] *Lyon in Mourning*, vol. ii.

memories. He never knew what he had done: to him the affair seemed perfectly natural.

The immediate objective was the island of Raasay, and the Prince's new companions (for MacEachain had been left behind) consisted of John Macleod (young Raasay), and his brothers, Captain Malcolm Macleod and Murdoch Macleod, with two boatmen. Murdoch had got a bullet through his shoulder at Culloden, and both the boatmen had been 'out.' Malcolm becomes our new historian.

They landed on Raasay in due course, but Charles did not like the place. It was a long, narrow island, easy to sweep with a ship's glasses; and there was a mysterious stranger loafing about there under the pretence of selling tobacco to the natives. Malcolm Macleod proposed to ensure this person's silence by shooting him through the head; Charles preferred to move back to Skye. So they made the crossing again, while he sang them "a merry Highland song," and spent the night in a cow-byre near Scorobeck.

The Prince for once began to show signs of nerves. He "started up" several times during the night, and, about 7 o'clock in the evening of the following day, he suddenly stepped out of the byre, seized the baggage, and started off down the road without a word. Most of the party remained where they were; but Malcolm Macleod hurried after him and, with an unceremonious "Give me that!" took the baggage away. "Your Royal Highness will pardon me to ask where you are going?" he inquired sarcastically. The Prince softened immediately: "I throw myself entirely in your hands." The only thing he refused to do was to remain in the byre. So they went on down the road together, making (at Charles's suggestion) for the country of the Mackinnons. It was agreed that he should pretend to be Malcolm's servant, so he pulled off his periwig and tied a dirty white napkin round his head instead, dragging it down over his eyes. Macleod feared that he was still recognizable. "This is an odd remarkable face I have got," exclaimed the Prince pettishly, "that nothing can disguise it."

They trudged on many weary miles, the Prince continually stopping to drink water, so that Macleod became quite alarmed, urging him to "qualify" it with a little brandy. No, said Charles, it would be all right—"only remember, Macleod, to piss after drinking, and it will do you no harm at all." When it appeared that the brandy bottle was nearly empty he insisted that his companion should drink what was left. He "walked very quickly," though he was but just recovering from dysentery. Here is a specimen of his small talk:

> "Macleod, do you not think that God Almighty has made this person of mine for doing some good yet? When I was in Italy, and dining at the King's table, very often the sweat would have been coming through my coat with the heat of the climate; and now that I am in a cold country, of a more piercing and trying climate, and exposed to different kinds of fatigues, I really find I agree equally with both."

At John Mackinnon's house they were hospitably received, and the old chief of the clan, disregarding the danger, took charge of the Prince and sent him by boat to the mainland. He landed at Borradale on July 10—his third visit. About this date Flora Macdonald was arrested and sent to the Tower of London; Kingsburgh also was imprisoned; both the Mackinnons were seized, and one of their boatmen who had brought the Prince over was tied to a tree and flogged; Malcolm Macleod was caught and subjected to gross ill-treatment at the hands of Captain Ferguson. But the secret was kept. The blood money still remained unclaimed.

The most that the Prince's enemies could discover was that he was back again on the mainland. A line of posts, or "little camps," was established from the head of Loch Hourn, on the coast, to the head of Loch Eil, so that it seemed impossible that he should break through inland to join his friends in the Cameron and Glengarry countries. None the less, it was determined to make the attempt, and the Prince set out on the 18th of July, accompanied by some of the Macdonalds and Donald Cameron of Glenpean. As they crossed the hills the soldiers' camps were in full view below them. At one place the Prince missed his footing, and was falling headlong down the steep hillside when the guide caught him by the foot; Glenpean at the same moment seized the guide with one hand and a bunch of shrub with the other, and so they all struggled back to safety. But it was a perilous passage.

That night (the 21st of July) they found they were through the cordon. But there were parties of soldiers all over the place, and on the very next day the Prince had the narrowest escape of all. They had just said good-bye to Donald Cameron of Glenpean when their new guide, Donald Macdonald, a Glengarry man, found that his purse had been stolen from him at the last stop. While he went back to get it the Prince hid by the side of the road. Hardly had he done so when a party of soldiers appeared within a few hundred yards and walked past his hiding-place. But for the incident of the lost purse, the fugitives must have been captured.

They entered the Glenmoriston country, and were presently met and taken charge of by the famous "eight men of Glenmoriston," two MacDonells, three Chisholms, a Macgregor, a Grant, and a Macmillan—men of the hills, robbers and outlaws perhaps, yet, as Bishop Forbes remarks, all of them boasting "the superlative honour to

despise £30,000." With this ragged escort, they reached
the cave in Glenmoriston, famous in the history of the
Prince's wanderings, where Charles slept upon a bed of
heather, "lulled asleep with the sweet murmurings of the
finest purling stream that could be, running by his bedside, within the grotto." This is at once the best authen-
ticated and the most romantic of all Prince Charlie's caves.
He remained there two days, moved on to another cave,
"equally romantic," and so, dodging up and down the
country (for it was never safe to keep still), always sending
out messengers to know if there was any French ship on
the coast, he at last got in touch with Macdonald of Lochgarry and Lochiel.

He had now many friends on the coast looking out for
him. On the 28th of August he paid off the "men of
Glenmoriston," and about a week later took refuge with
Cluny Macpherson in that strange little hut, on the side of
a mountain, known to history (and all readers of R. L.
Stevenson) as "Cluny's Cage." Cluny, of course, apart
from his loyalty, could never refuse Charles anything.
When the Prince begged a favour, he said, "an angel
could not resist."

The vigilance of the Hanoverians was now somewhat
relaxed. The camp at Fort Augustus had been broken up
and Campbell's militia disbanded. On the 13th of
September the Prince, at Cluny's Cage, heard that there
were two French ships at Loch-na-Nuagh. He started for
the coast at once, accompanied by Lochiel, Lochgarry,
and others. It is pleasant to know that his old friends
were with him at the end. Cluny met them at the head
of Loch Arkaig, and they travelled all day to Borradale,
where the Prince got on board the French privateer
L'Heureux.

They weighed anchor shortly after midnight on the
19th of September, and, aided by a convenient fog, sailed

INTERIOR OF THE CAVE IN GLENMORISTON
From a sketch by Alex Ross

safely past the English ships and so away to the coast of France.

Silence fell upon the Highlands. The hills, all purple and glowing with their September colouring, seemed utterly deserted. Only here and there the head of some fugitive might be raised for a moment above the heather —to duck down quickly again at the sight of red coats in the valley. Along the main roads trudged parties of soldiers, militia, Campbell levies, searching the villages, hunting down wounded Jacobites, burning the lairds' houses—making an end of the clans. They broke the power of the chiefs, they harried Episcopalian and Catholic priests indiscriminately, they destroyed religion and education, they forbade the wearing of the kilt. The Whigs had always maintained that the Highlanders were savages; now they were doing their best to make them so.

John Macdonald, the eighteenth-century footman, has told us in his memoirs [1] how he and his brothers and sisters, children of a well-to-do Highlander who had lost his life and all his possessions in Prince Charlie's cause, were forced to beg their way from Urquhart to Edinburgh in September 1745. Local Whigs would repulse these starving children from their doors. "The poor Highlanders," says Macdonald, "were despised at that time by the Scots in general, of the other party, more than the devils in hell."

The cruelties associated with the name of "Butcher" Cumberland had begun, as we have seen, at Culloden. He gave no quarter to a gallant foe. I agree with Miss Audrey Cunningham [2] that there seems to be no reason to doubt the evidence of Bishop Forbes, who has included in his *Lyon in Mourning* first-hand accounts of some of the worst

[1] *Travels in Various Parts of Europe, Asia, and Africa*, by John Macdonald London, 1790).   [2] *The Loyal Clans* (Cambridge, 1932).

atrocities committed by Cumberland's troops. Immediately after the battle there was a search made through the surrounding houses; wounded Highlanders were dragged out and shot or clubbed to death. A barn where a number of prisoners were collected was set on fire. We have the evidence of several eyewitnesses that parties moved about the battlefield deliberately killing the wounded. The dead were stripped naked and left lying there for days.

On the very evening of the battle, when the sound of the firing had hardly died down, it chanced that Lady Findlater had occasion to drive in her coach across Culloden Moor towards Inverness. And if it be asked how a lady came to be there I can only explain that this strong-minded woman, with her husband, who was a prominent Whig, had followed Cumberland all the way from Aberdeen and had stood and watched the battle from afar. As she crossed that tragic field the work of the pillagers had already begun, and the Highland dead lay scattered in every direction, "stripped of all their clothes." One among them, Ranald Macdonald of Bellfinlay, was still alive, and to him Bishop Forbes applied, some months later, for evidence as to whether Lady Findlater was really in the coach. Macdonald said that as he lay there, unable to rise for his wounds, he "saw a coach and six drive over the field towards Inverness and approaching so near the spot where I was lying that I began to be afraid they would drive over my naked body, which made me stir a little and look up." He saw ladies in the coach, but would not swear to their identity. He adds, however, that it "came so near me that the coachman made a lick at me with his whip as if I had been a dog."

There is something in that simple, instinctive action by the Findlater coachman more horribly significant than all the calculated cruelties of the Government or the worst excesses of the troops.

CHAPTER XIII

IN EXILE

In this book, as should surely be clear from the title, the Prince we are primarily concerned with is the Bonnie Prince Charlie of the Forty-five. That was the great effort of his career. It was a failure, but a failure that most people nowadays would agree in labelling a victory —one of the classic instances in human history of victory in defeat.

I have said that there was a silence in the Highland heather. So there was, but always with the breath of his passing still there. The great romantic tradition of which this simple-minded young man of action was the unconscious founder still lived and flourished under the trampling boots of the southern invaders, and was to burst into bloom half a century later, with a riot of music and song, idealist tartans, and impossible Floras, and a whole new springtime of romance, which we may sneer at if we like as early nineteenth century sentimentalism, but which is really a hardy, imperishable growth, deeply embedded in English and Scottish soil and likely to outlive most of our modern sentimentalities. From this point of view— indeed, from any point of view—the later period of Prince Charlie's life does not greatly matter. It is a perfectly sound popular instinct which thinks of him always as a young man, ignoring those weary, wasted, insignificant years. There is little to be gained from the contemplation of a man of action who has no longer anything to do.

Landing at Roscoff, in Brittany, he drove to Morlaix

on the 10th of October, and immediately found himself immersed in correspondence concerning the trustworthiness of this man or that, the removal of this or that servant, the alleged discontents of his brother Henry (who was still devoted to him), and all the miserable intrigues with which James III seemed invariably to be surrounded. The brothers met and embraced. Charles sought an interview with Louis XV, and presently had the honour of supping with the King and Mme de Pompadour at Fontainebleau. But he was more adept at imitating the call of the plover than at pleasing pretty ladies like the Pompadour. For three years, as Andrew Lang has said, "he broke himself on the French politicians." It was sheer waste of time. They offered pensions for himself and his brother, whereas all he asked for was a force of twenty thousand regulars for the reconquest of Scotland. In this attitude he was supported by Lochiel, who was dragging out his few remaining years as an exile in France.

Another distinguished refugee was Lord George Murray, who arrived in Rome about the beginning of April 1747. Charles's feelings towards him had not softened—though he had made a kindly enough reference to him in conversation with Kingsburgh at Skye—and he now wrote from Paris to his father in Rome urging that Murray should be forcibly detained there until he had justified himself. "It would be of the most dangerous consequences," he argued, "if such a Divill was not secured immediately in some castle, where he might be at his ease, but without being able to escape, or have the liberty of pen or paper." In fact, he had persuaded himself that Murray was a traitor. In another letter he made the absurd suggestion that there had been collusion between Lord George Murray and Murray of Broughton, who were sworn enemies. James sent a very proper reply in which he declined to detain Murray against his will, described him as "penitent" and "owning his faults," and begged his son to give his old comrade in arms "a good reception" when the latter arrived in Paris. But when Murray reached that city two months later Charles not only refused to see him, but sent a message requesting him to depart—which he did. There is little excuse for such conduct. But it was all part of Charles's attitude at this time. He clung desperately to the hope of another campaign overseas. His eyes were turned always towards England. Hence his refusal to settle down—to accept the manners or religion of the Continent. And he was coldly determined that if he ever took the field again it would be without the advice or assistance of an expert in retreats.

His brother Henry, not unnaturally, took a different view. Henry was an earnest Catholic, soon to become a Cardinal. Charles, it was increasingly evident, wished to be regarded as a member of the Church of England. He was not a religiously minded man; in any case, London would have seemed to him worth a Mass. In April 1747 Henry quietly left Paris for Rome. A few weeks later it was announced that he had taken the Cardinal's hat— to the great joy of most of the Jacobites at James's little Court, to the supreme disgust of Charles. "As I am fully convinced of the sincerity and solidity of his vocation," wrote James in explanation to his elder son, "I should think it a resisting the will of God, and acting directly against my conscience, if I should pretend to constrain him."

We can imagine Charles's contemptuous comment as he threw this letter aside. It was, he declared, the worst blow his cause in England had received since Culloden. For himself, he swore never to return to Rome. He became every day more aggressively English. Old Sheridan was dead of an apoplexy (after a violent quarrel

with Elcho, who was also in exile), but young Sheridan
was with him, and O'Sullivan and Kelly, the Irish priest;
and they seem to have encouraged him in his attitude
of defiance towards the French Court, which his father
could only suppose was adopted in order to curry favour
in England. If so there was reason in it. The Treaty
of Aix-la-Chapelle was impending; he must have realized
that for the moment he could hope for nothing from
France.

But while he quarrelled with the French Court his
attraction for the women seems to have been as strong as
ever. Two of them, the Princesse de Talmond and Mme
d'Aiguillon, almost fought over him. The Minister
d'Argenson—who refused all Charles's requests, but
always had a sneaking affection for him—introduced the
subject into a play which he left behind in manuscript
when he died. The story did the Prince no harm. If
he had been another Casanova eighteenth-century France
would have thought nothing of it. But since he had
the habits of an ordinary English or Scottish squire of
the period they mistook him for a drunkard. The charge
crops up again and again. It rests mainly upon the
evidence of Walton and Mann, the English agents,
who had depicted him as a cripple and a half-wit in
his youth, and now, for the same reasons, would have
him a moral and physical wreck. Yet he lived to the
age of sixty-eight, and never had a serious breakdown
till near the end. Admittedly this third Charles had
neither the strong religious principles of Charles I nor
the comfortable philosophy of Charles II to sustain him.
The Bonnie Prince Charlie of Jacobite tradition can
have been no ordinary man; but he was ordinary in the
sense of having few mental reserves. By nature and
upbringing he was one who naturally expressed himself
in action. And when, at a comparatively early age, he

IN LATER LIFE
Pompeo Batoni
National Portrait Gallery

228

found himself, after a few desperate but futile flutterings, condemned to a life of idleness, he did what most men of his type would have done in such circumstances—he rather ran to seed. That, on all the evidence, seems a fairer description of the change which presently began to appear in him than the commonly accepted picture of a confirmed drunkard.

In the meantime he dressed magnificently, laughed in the face of the Court, and was followed everywhere he went by an admiring crowd of Parisians. In view of the peace with England, it was essential to get rid of him. The French King offered him any pension he liked if only he would go. His own father wrote commanding him "to obey his Most Christian Majesty instantly." At last an order was signed for his arrest. As his carriage passed along the Rue Saint-Honoré to the Opéra sympathetic voices from the crowd warned him to turn back. He went on, and was duly seized by the guard, dragged down a long passage, and relieved of his sword and pistols. He had expected this. "The manner is a little too violent" was his quiet comment. They bound him—but with a crimson silk cord, specially provided!— and carried him out to a coach and conveyed him to the Château of Vincennes, he behaving with perfect coolness throughout. Only when his gaolers had left him alone with a few friends did he burst into a torrent of reproaches. Even when hunted in the Highlands, he exclaimed, he was never thrown into gaol—"like a wild beast, he had at least ground to range over." He never forgot this insult.

A week later they escorted him politely to the Italian frontier, and left him there to his own devices. He had told his escort jokingly that he would probably be heard of next at Constantinople. In fact, he hired a chaise and drove to Avignon. Of course, he had no business there; and he further annoyed the ecclesiastical authorities by

attempting to introduce into the Papal city the rough
English sport of boxing. He was urged to depart,
and on the 28th of February, 1749, he rode away from
the town with one companion, Henry Goring, and for
five years wandered about Europe in disguise, no doubt
encountering innumerable adventures, but utterly lost
to the official world. He wrote occasionally to his father,
reassuring him as to his health, but giving no address.
Rumours that he was ill or dying were eagerly swallowed
by the English agents abroad and forwarded to St
James's; but there was no truth in them. What is certain
is that he went first to Paris, and that the French Ministers,
in spite of their professions of ignorance, must have known
that he was there. He was protected by the Princesse
de Talmond and at least two other French ladies—Mlle
Ferrand and Mme de Vasse. Wild schemes were simmer-
ing in his head.

On some date between the 12th and the 16th of
September, 1750, that charming English hostess Lady
Primrose was giving a party at her house in Essex Street,
Strand. There was "a pretty large company" present,
and a cheerful clatter of tongues, we may be sure, for in
eighteenth-century London the art of conversation was
still a living thing. The hostess herself had sat down
with some of her guests to a game of cards. Suddenly
the servant announced another visitor. The name was
unknown to Lady Primrose, but she rose politely to greet
a youngish-looking man of distinguished appearance, and
as she did so "she thought the cards would have dropped
from her hands." She had recognized him immediately.
Controlling her emotions with an effort, she asked him
when he had crossed to England and how long he meant
to stay. He answered affably, but vaguely. It happened
that while they talked he stood immediately beneath a
large portrait of Prince Charles Edward Stuart which

hung above the chimney-piece (for Lady Primrose made no secret of her Jacobite leanings), and this must have added not a little to her embarrassment. As soon as she could she got rid of the other guests, and had then to endure the remarks of her servants, who commented upon the extraordinary resemblance between their lady's visitor and the picture of the Young Pretender.

This dramatic visit to London seems to have been Charles's own idea. Certainly Lady Primrose was not the only prominent Jacobite who was quite unprepared for it. She now sent for Dr King, the principal of St Mary Hall, Oxford, and a leading sympathizer. King interviewed the Prince, and was amazed to hear of the madcap scheme which had brought him to London. He had been negotiating in Antwerp for the purchase of twenty-six thousand muskets. The idea was to seize the Tower of London! He had brought over with him a certain Colonel Brett, and in company with this optimist he traversed the streets of London, entirely without disguise, inspected the defences of the Tower, and—if we may believe subsequent gossip—came to the conclusion that one of the gates could be blown in with a petard. There was a meeting of his friends, including the Duke of Beaufort and the Earl of Westmorland, when the Prince is said to have declared that if they could raise four thousand men he would place himself at their head, and—in modern parlance—damn the consequences.

All of which does undoubtedly sound as though he had been drinking too much. But it must be remembered that for the history of this strange visit we have nothing but gossip to go upon, and that largely from hostile sources.[1] The significant fact is that after one

[1] Dr King's version of it was written after he had gone over to the Government side.

short week in London Charles dropped the idea and
went back to the Continent. It was an escapade after
his own heart. We can believe that he thoroughly
enjoyed prowling about the London streets—it was
almost as exciting as his adventures in the heather. How
far he meant it seriously we shall never know. But it
is a fact—for he has told us himself—that during this
visit he solemnly abjured the "Romish religion" and
"did embrace that of the Church of England as by law
established in the Thirty-nine Articles, in which I hope
to live and die." This declaration is said to have been
made "in the new church in the Strand"; but neither
at St Martin's-in-the-Fields, St Mary-le-Strand, nor
St Clement Danes is there any official record of it.[1]
It was a purely political move.

The chief interest of this London visit for the student
of Charles's character is the proof which it supplies of his
persistent, inherent boyishness. His character had been
formed in the Highlands. Whatever else happened to
him—political disappointments, the misery of enforced
inaction—he remained what he was then, a high-
spirited young man in his early twenties. Politically the
result was the singularly futile Elibank Plot, which came
to a head in 1752. Alexander Murray, brother of Lord
Elibank, was to attack St James's Palace and kidnap (or,
as some said, assassinate) the royal family; Archibald
Cameron and others were to stir up the Highlands.
Charles gave these plotters some encouragement, though
it is unthinkable that either he or his father, who was
still alive, would have countenanced the murder of King
George. The appointment of that old, over-cautious
Jacobite the Earl Marischal as Prussian Ambassador

---

[1] I am greatly indebted to Sir Charles Petrie's paper on *The Elibank Plot*,
1752–53, read before the Royal Historical Society on January 8, 1931. He has
carefully examined all the authorities for Charles's visit to London, and the
genesis of the subsequent Elibank Plot.

to the Court of France gave rise to more false hopes. (Frederick of Prussia meant no more by it than a little timely twisting of the British lion's tail.) The Plot came to an end with the arrest and execution of Cameron in 1752.

It may be that Charles visited London again. Hume says he was there in 1753, but the details which he gives are those of the visit of 1750, described above. Philip Thicknesse mentions an alleged visit in 1754. On the other hand, Glengarry, who knew all about the Elibank Plot (he was probably a Government spy), definitely asserts that the Prince—"thank God!"—did not venture himself in London. Andrew Lang's suggestion that he may have gone to stay with Mme de Mezières at Godalming seems to have been finally disposed of by Sir Charles Petrie. In fact, there is no reason to suppose that he ever visited England again.

Back on the Continent with his dead ambitions and nothing to look forward to but a life of perpetual marking time and a society which was becoming increasingly distasteful, his thoughts turned at last to the black-eyed Scottish girl of Bannockburn. He wrote to Clementina Walkinshaw, reminding her of her promise. She set out immediately and joined him, probably at Ghent, in 1752. It was a bad move. He was always clumsy in his dealings with women. Clementina, whose sister had but recently been appointed a lady-in-waiting to the Princess of Wales, was regarded with suspicion by the Jacobite exiles. At first all went well with the pair, but Charles was no marrying man, and the seeds of trouble were there. Goring, in particular, objected to her presence, and thus Charles quarrelled with one of his few remaining friends. Yet less than a month after Clementina's child was born their relations were such that he swore he would have no more to do with her!

He was becoming embittered against the world. Spies followed him wherever he went, his father did nothing but lecture him, he was forced to apply for money to his friends—even to Cluny Macpherson, who can have had little to give. Lord Elcho, still an exile, hastened to visit Clementina and listen to her tale of woe.[1] James Dawkins, the archæologist, and once his friend, accused him of leading an irregular, debauched life. The Earl Marischal, who had always underestimated him, wrote a stern letter. "My heart is broke enough," replied Charles, "without that you should finish it." In fact, almost every one was tired of him. He was becoming as unattractive as a bedraggled eagle in a small cage. He added to the score against him at the French Court by declining indignantly to accept a military command against the English in the attack on Minorca in 1757. "I will no longer serve as a mere bugbear," he said. Which, as Andrew Lang remarks, "showed a just appreciation of French policy."

In 1760 Clementina left him and took refuge in a convent, taking her little daughter with her. She wrote to him excusing her conduct and alleging that she was "always in perpetual dread of my life from your violent passions." She goes on to suggest that "you are not yourself" and "your head is gone again." One would suppose that he had not long to live.

His father, however, preceded him to the grave. James died on the 1st of January, 1766. Obviously it was no longer possible for Charles to maintain his refusal to visit Rome. He arrived there in the following month, travelling under the name of Douglas, and Mann, the

---

[1] She told him that Charles often thrashed her fifty times a day with a stick and was so jealous that " he invariably surrounded their bed with chairs placed on tables, and on the chairs little bells, so if anyone approached during the night the bells would be set a-ringing."

English agent, records with disgust the cordiality of his reception by all classes. The Jacobite exiles hailed him as "Charles III, their Sovereign." His old friend and secretary, Lumisden, says that he "charms every one that approaches him." His brother Henry hastened to make friends, and the two appeared together in the streets of Rome, as in the old days, seated in the same carriage. Only the Pope remained strictly 'correct,' and wrote to Henry pointing out that cardinals should give the right-hand seat in their carriages to nobody but crowned heads.

Yet it is pleasant to recognize that for the moment life took on a brighter hue for Prince Charles. Here, among the scenes of his boyhood, he seemed to recapture something of his youthful zest. He became a regular attendant at the opera, which he loved, and, though he still disliked social functions, he was amiable to those he met. The English Ambassador at Naples,[1] more honest than most of them, describes him as "rather handsome" and "good-natured," though his face was "ruddy and full of pimples." The shooting season had begun. Though still supposed to be addicted to "the nasty bottle," Charles was constantly out with his gun, among the hills which he had so often shot over in his boyhood. It would be interesting to know whether this alleged dipsomaniac still succeeded in "papping them down" as he did in Scotland. "His complexion is of the fair tint," wrote an English lady then in Rome, "his eyes blue, his hair light brown, and the contour of his face a long oval; he is by no means thin, has a noble person and a graceful manner." His dress, when she saw him, was "scarlet lace with broad gold lace."

About the year 1770 the unhappy idea entered his head of making a matrimonial alliance, in order to provide

---

[1] This was Sir William Hamilton, a judge of feminine if not of masculine good looks, though he had not yet brought his beautiful Emma out to Naples.

England with a suitable Stuart heir. In 1771 he went to Paris and, while living there *incognito*, began to put out feelers. The Princess Louise of Stolberg (a noble but impoverished house) was indicated as a suitable victim. She was a blonde of middle height, "with deep blue eyes, a nose slightly turned up, complexion dazzling fair." She seems to have made the sacrifice very willingly. The marriage was first performed by proxy at Paris, and then Charles returned to Italy. Louise—like Clementina Sobieski before her—made the journey through Austrian territory to Bologna, and at Macerata met her bridegroom in person, and was formally united to him on Good Friday 1772—not a very auspicious date.

The rest of the story is squalid enough. An empty title of royalty did not conceal the greater emptiness of their life. Among the first to greet them in Rome were Clementina Walkinshaw and her daughter Charlotte! The Pope refused them royal honours; at Florence, whither they moved in 1774, it was the same. Louise was young, and she took lovers—first Alfieri, then Gehegan, an Irishman. Charles, his suspicions aroused, broke into her room one day, and there was a disgraceful scene. She seems to have been an unpleasant little baggage. Yet when she appealed to the Pope and Cardinal Henry they at once assumed that Charles was in the wrong, and she set out for Rome to seek their protection with her two lovers seated on the box! Half Charles's pension was allotted to her, so that he was compelled to reduce his establishment.

He had still ten more years to live, this "poor vision of a man," as the English agent at Florence calls him, who still keeps a box of sequins under his bed against the day when he may be suddenly called upon to make the journey to England. The agent thinks that the Secretary of State, to whom his letter is addressed, will find this last

BONNIE PRINCE CHARLIE
John Pettie

236

detail highly "laughable." In fact, his health was failing. He suffered from dropsy, shortness of breath, and a running sore in the leg, and felt very ill and miserable. In 1784, despairing of recovering his wife, he sent for Clementina's daughter Charlotte, legitimated her, and made her Duchess of Albany. It was the best thing he could have done. A cheerful, healthy, good-natured girl, she remained with him for the rest of his life, composed his latest quarrel with his brother Henry, watched over his health, and prevented his visitors from exciting him by talking about the Highlands.

Yet it is into those Highland mists, encircling the distant isles of Uist and Skye, that his uneasy spirit seems gradually to fade as death approaches him. From his gilt-upholstered bed in the Italian mansion where he gasped out his latest breath on the last day of January 1788 we can imagine his soul taking flight to the far-off land of his adoption, where he had almost succeeded in overthrowing a dynasty, and, failing that, had set up something greater instead. There in the little cave in Glenmoriston, or in the "clift of a rock" on Ouia, he had been able to express the best that was in him. There in the Highlands he would be received and understood and welcomed. There, indeed, his spirit remains for all time.

INDEX

Home, John, quoted, 53, 97, 116, 172 *n.*, 189, 201 *n.*
Hume, David, quoted, 111, 232
Huske, General John, 178

INNSBRUCK, rescue of Princess Clementina at, 11–23
Invergarry Castle, the Prince at, 205
Inverness, Cope's retirement to, 84; held by Loudoun, 159, 160; Jacobite retreat to, 186–189, 192; halt at, 189; skirmishes near, 190; the Prince's difficulties at, 193–194
Inversnaid Barracks, raid on, 84.
Inverurie, skirmish at, 160–162
Iubhard, island of, the Prince's stay on, 211–212

JACOBITE army, morals of, 113; pay of, 117; recruits for, 122, 123–125; cracking morale of, 193–194
Jacobite cause, injured by royal quarrels, 39; in 1743, 56; in Scotland, 52, 53; and Walpole, 50, 51
Jacobite "Concert," or Association, formation and schemes of, 53–54; activities of, 55
Jacobite 'defeatists,' secret meetings of, 125
Jacobites, English, 50; Scottish, alarm of, 60; the hunting down of, 223–224
James III, 26, 43, 56, 60, 164; and the Pope, 33, 40–41; marriage plans, marriage, and married life of, 13, 30, 32, 33, 37–42; letter from, on Prince Charles, 49–50; and death of George I, 51; on Prince Charles, 70; Prince Charles proclaims himself Regent for, 85; and Lord George Murray, 226–227; attitude of, to Cardinal York, 227; order of, to Prince Charles, 229; death of, 234
Jenkins's Ear, War of, 52, 53
Jenny —, share of, in rescue of Princess Clementina, 15, 17 *et seq.*; later fate of, 33
Johnson, Dr Samuel and the Forty-five, 158
Johnstone, Chevalier de, quoted, 102, 113–114, 117, 124, 145, 146, 169, 172, 180, 181, 183, 201 *n.*, 206–207

KEITH, garrison captured at, 193
Keith, George, Earl Marischal—*see* Marischal, the Earl
Kelly, Father, confessor to Prince Charles, 58–59, 228
Kelly, George, 58, 61; urges a stand, 136
Kendal, Jacobite forces at, 121, 143, 144
Ker, Lord Mark, 181
Kilmarnock, Earl of, 117, 121, 169, 178
Kilmarnock, Countess of, 178; and Hawley, 169
King, Dr, interview of, with the Prince, 231; quoted, 231 *n.*
Kinlochmoidart, guide from, for the Prince, 208

LANCASTER, 121; Prince Charles's wish to stand at, 143, 164
Lang, Andrew, quoted, 49, 56, 65, 133, 142, 226, 233, 234
Lesmahagow, 153
Ligonier, General, advance of, 118, 119
Linton, Lord (later Earl of Traquair), 53
Lion, H.M.S., engagement of, with the *Elizabeth,* 62–63
Liria, Duke of (later Duke of Berwick), and Prince Charles, 43–44
Loch-na-Nuagh, the Prince at, 68.
Lockhart, George, and the *Lockhart Papers,* quoted, 41, 70
London, the Jacobite objective, 111, 114; defence of, 118; danger of attempt on, 132; the Prince's visit to, in 1750, 230–231
London Gazette, quoted, 153.
Loudoun, Lord, 98, 159–160, 187, 188, 190, 194; regiment raised by, 82
Louis XV, 16–17, 112; and Jacobite cause, 56, 136, 159; the Prince's supper with, 226; efforts of, to get rid of the Prince, 228–229
Lovat, Lord, 53, 69, 133, 160, 205; letter from, to the Prince, 83–84; son of, joining the Prince, 160
Lucan, Lord, 31
Lumisden, Andrew, quoted, 105, 178

INDEX

Portree, parting of the Prince and Flora Macdonald at, 218
Preston, 121, 143
Preston, General George, 88
Prestonpans, battle of, 99–108, 130, 166, 182, 202; Carlyle's impressions of, 109; effect of, 111–112
Primrose, Lady, the Prince's dramatic visit to, in 1750, 230

RAMSAY, CHEVALIER, quoted, 36–37
Robertson of Struan, joins the Prince, 86
Rome, Prince Charles in, 234–235, 236
Ruthven, attempt to seize barracks at, 84
Ruthven of Badenoch, 206; the end of the Forty-five at, 206–207
Rutlidge, Walter, 61

SAXE, MARSHAL, 55, 57, 58
Scalpa, the Prince at, 209–210, 211, 212
Scotland, attitude of, to Jacobite cause, 116
Scott, Captain John, 76–78
Seaforth, Earl of, 160
Seaforth, Countess of, 160
Sempill, Lord, 57, 59; mistaken optimism of, 53, 56
Seton, 99
Seven Men of Moidart, the, 61, 64, 85, 135, 136
Shap, brush with Cumberland at, 144–145
Sheridan, Sir Thomas, 58, 61, 69, 110, 163, 194, 205; and the Prince's couch, 66; and the retreat from Derby, 137; death of, 227–228; quoted, 179
Sheridan, —, son of the above, 228.
Skye, the Prince's escape to, 216–218, 219
Skyring, Mrs, 126
Sobieski, Prince James, 13, 14
Sobieski, Princess, 13, 19, 28
Sobieski, Princess Clementina, 163; rescue and marriage of, 13–28, 33, 157, 235; later years of, 37–42; death of, 47
South Uist, wanderings of the Prince and his followers in, 214

Spey, the, Cumberland's advance to, 192–194
Stafford, Mr, tutor to Prince Charles, 42
Stanford, Mr, and his horse, 128
Stanhope, Lord, quoted, 125–126
Stapleton, Brigadier, 190, 191, 194, 206
Stewart, Alexander, 188
Stirling, 86; Cope's camp at, 82
Stirling Castle, siege of, 162, 163, 167, 180–181, 182, 183
Stolberg, Princess Louise of, marriage of, with the Prince, and after-life, 236–237
Stornoway, the Prince's journey to, and return from, 209, 210–211
Strange, Sir Robert, quoted, 197
Strickland, Francis, tutor to Prince Charles, 49, 61
Stuart of Ardshiel, 76, 84, 87, 110; colour-bearer at Culloden, 79
Stuart, Colonel John Roy, 84, 121, 146
Stuart, Hon. John, 53
Stuart, Prince Charles Edward :
Appearance, dress, and portraits of, 35, 68, 71, 74, 92–93, 122, 124, 129, 156, 200, 230, 235
Biographical references to: birth and birthplace, 33, 148; first letter of, 34; education and religion of, 36, 37, 38, 40, 41, 227, 231–232; and the siege of Gaëta, 43–45, 47; 'grand tour' of, 48–49; Jacobite summons to, and journey to Gravelines, 56–57; last chance of, 59; decision and plans of, 60–61; passage of, on the *Doutelle*, 61–64; contemporary accounts of, 70–72; at Borradale, 73, 207–208, 220, 222; landing of, at Eriskay, 64–66; activities of, on landing in Scotland, 66–68; and the raising of the standard at Glenfinnan, 74, 76, 78–80; progress of, with his Highlanders, 76; James III's commission to, 79; movements and growing strength of, 83, 111–112, 114, 116, 117; proclaims himself Regent, 85; relations of, with Lord George Murray (*q.v.*), tension in, 85, 88–89, 120, 133, 137, 141, 148, 163–165, 196, 226–227;

245